DRAWINGS
FRENCH IMPRESSIONISTS

DRAWINGS
FRENCH IMPRESSIONISTS

by
Bohumír Mráz

3M Books
St. Paul, Minnesota
1985

FRENCH IMPRESSIONISTS: Drawings
by Bohumír Mráz
Designer: Václav Ševčík

Editor, English language edition: Pamela Espeland
Translated from the German by Christa Tiefenbacher-Hudson
Designers, English language edition: Evans-Smith & Skubic, Incorporated

Library of Congress Cataloging in Publication Data

Mráz, Bohumír.
  Drawings: French impressionists.

  Bibliography: p.
  1. Drawing, French—Catalogs. 2. Impressionism
(Art)—France—Catalogs. 3. Drawing—19th century—
France—Catalogs. I. Title
NC246.M73 1985   741.944'074   85-14712
ISBN 0-88159-804-6

© ODEON, Prague, 1985
English Language Edition
© Minnesota Mining & Mfg. Co., 1985
All Rights Reserved

Distributed to the trade by the Putnam Publishing Group
Printed in Czechoslovakia

CONTENTS

Notes on the Collotype Process

To achieve the most accurate reproductions possible, the publishers of this volume have elected to use a special photographic process called *collotype*. This expensive and old-fashioned printing method was invented in 1855 and put into commercial use in 1868. At most, it can produce only a few thousand copies, yet because of its ability to render fine detail it remains in demand for short runs of fine art prints of illustrations and for limited editions of books.

A collotype is made on a sheet of ground glass coated with bichromated gelatin. The plate is first dried in an oven until the gelatin reticulates into a pattern of almost microscopic cracks. A continuous-tone negative is then held up to the plate and light is passed through both the plate and the negative, causing the gelatin to harden in direct proportion to the tones of the negative.

Following this step the plate is washed to remove the bichromate and treated with a glycerine solution that moistens the areas which remained less hard after their exposure to light. A greasy lithographic ink is then rolled over the plate. The ink is repelled by the moist areas but accepted by the tiny reticulation cracks of the dry, hardened areas. Finally, paper is pressed against the plate and the image is transferred.

The collotype process is unsuitable for long print runs due to the fact that the delicate gelatin surface begins to slowly deteriorate after approximately one thousand copies are made. Without the gelatin, however, it would not be possible to reproduce with such accuracy the detailing and shading of the original work of art. Thus, while the process does not lend itself to mass production, it does result in superb prints that capture the beauty and intensity of the French Impressionists' drawings.

For this volume, the collotype process was used to reproduce each of the 56 black-and-white plates. The 32 color plates and the 13 illustrations within the text were reproduced by the more usual method of offset printing.

IMPRESSIONS OF IMPRESSIONISM

One is too much preoccupied with what one sees and hears in Paris, however strong-minded one may be, and what I do here will at least have the merit of resembling nobody else because it will simply be the impression of what I alone have felt.

—Claude Monet, Le Havre, 1868

In 1874 the French art critic Louis Leroy wrote an article for the satiric journal *Le Charivari* in which he mockingly branded Claude Monet, Auguste Renoir, Edgar Degas, Alfred Sisley, Camille Pissarro, Paul Cézanne, Berthe Morisot, and twenty-three of their colleagues as "Impressionists." Little did Leroy suspect that he had coined the name of a new artistic movement, a name that many of the artists themselves soon adopted. Ironically, in a matter of decades the "Impressionist" paintings Leroy so heartily disdained became some of the best-loved and most widely recognized in the history of Western art.

The first Impressionist group exhibition opened on April 15, 1874 in spacious rooms near the fashionable Boulevard des Capucines that had recently been vacated by the photographer Nadar. It comprised 165 paintings by thirty artists, many of whom had known one another since the early 1860s. They had first talked of organizing a group exhibit late in that decade, when their paintings were being rejected annually by the jury of the official Salon, but the Franco-Prussian War of 1870-71 had interrupted their plans. After the war—and the death of their young comrade, Frédéric Bazille—Monet took the lead in bringing them together again.

They called themselves the *Société anonyme des artistes, peintres, sculpteurs, graveurs, etc.* (Anonymous Society of Artists, Painters, Sculptors, Engravers, etc.), and the exhibit lasted four weeks. From the beginning it caused a sensation. Critics and the public alike were shocked by what they saw, and the 3,500 people who attended, attracted by articles like the one written by Leroy, came primarily to be amused. Most of the other serious critics flatly refused to review the show.

Leroy's caustic comments appeared in *Le Charivari* on April 25, 1874 and was the first published piece on the exhibit. Entitled "Exhibition of the Impressionists," it was written under the guise of a gallery tour by the author and M. Joseph Vincent, a medal-winning landscape painter. As the two pause before painting after painting, Vincent becomes increasingly agitated by the "sloppiness of tone" and "messy composition" until, faced with Monet's *Impression: Sunrise*, he completely loses his senses:

> "Impression—I was certain of it" [Vincent said]. "I was just telling myself that, since I was impressed, there had to be some impression in it . . . and what freedom, what ease of workmanship! Wallpaper in its embryonic state is more finished than that seascape."
>
> In vain [Leroy noted] I sought to revive his expiring reason . . . but the horrible fascinated him. (Rewald, *History of Impressionism*, p. 323.)

As it happened, Monet himself was responsible for the label that Leroy seized upon to characterize the entire movement. When pressed to provide titles for certain of his paintings for the exhibition catalog, he had replied, "Just put *Impression*."

Leroy's sentiments were echoed by other critics as well. An American writer referred to "that highly comical exhibition," and J. Claretie, a well-known reviewer of the annual Salon, agreed: "M. Monet . . . Pissarro, Mlle Morisot, etc., appear to have declared war on beauty." The tone of this criticism so alarmed Berthe Morisot's mother that she asked her daughter's former teacher, Joseph Guichard, whether the situation was really that bad. He sadly replied: "I became anguished upon seeing the works of your daughter in those pernicious surroundings. I said to myself, 'One doesn't live with impunity among madmen.'"

Various friends of the artists came to their defense, if somewhat less than enthusiastically. Philippe Burty and Armand Silvestre both wrote favorable reviews, but even their praise was not unqualified. Jules Castagnary, writing in *Le Siècle* on April 29, 1874, acknowledged the considerable talents of Monet, Pissarro, Renoir, Sisley, and Morisot and then added this not-so-gentle scolding:

> The strongest among them . . . will have recognized that while there are subjects which lend themselves to a rapid "impression," to the appearance of a sketch, there are others and in much greater numbers that demand a more precise impression. . . . Those painters who, continuing their course, will have perfected their draftsmanship, will abandon *impression* as an art really too superficial for them.
> (Rewald, *History of Impressionism*, p. 330.)

W hat was it about the Impressionists' work that outraged the public and dismayed even their friends? In short, just about everything: their subject matter, their technique, and their use of color. Although there was great diversity of style among the works that Leroy termed "Impressionist," the ones which got the most attention and elicited the loudest outcry all differed radically from what French bourgeois society considered "good" painting.

This large, aesthetically untrained middle class thronged the Paris Salon each year to acquire culture and purchase works of art to decorate their living rooms, and hundreds of financially dependent artists catered to what these patrons wanted to buy. To the bourgeoisie, the Impressionists were simply bad painters who were incapable of accurately reproducing the appearance of the real world. The people were used to seeing—in fact, demanded—canvases containing figures and objects that looked genuine enough to touch. The Impressionists presented a serious challenge to what they understood as "Art," and while some applauded the artists' freedom from convention, all were upset.

In the Salons of the 1860s and 1870s, history painting—a category which also included religious, mythological, and literary themes—still held sway as the most noble subject matter. Large, ponderous canvases depicted great Napoleonic battles, the death of Julius Caesar, nymphs reclining languidly in forests, and Adam and Eve finding the body of their murdered son, Abel. Another type of history painting had also become popular during this time in response to the public's taste for genre scenes. Artists fabricated "little histories" showing private moments of famous historical figures. For example, Joan of Arc was pictured handcuffed in her jail cell, eyes cast appealingly heavenward, rather than marching at the head of an army or dying nobly at the stake.

Actually, the public embraced almost any genre subject: sad-eyed children, mothers and their infants, haymaking in the country, a brawl at a local tavern. The sentimental, often moralizing anecdotes such paintings contained, and the small, intimate sizes of the canvases, made them ideal for the middle-class drawing room. Many Salon painters succeeded solely on the basis of their ability to tell a story; their artistic skills were secondary. Landscape painting also gained favor around the middle of the century, and there was general acceptance of the so-called "realist" landscapes of the Barbizon artists who, like the Impressionists, chose to paint out-of-doors.

The Impressionists' subject matter, in contrast, consisted of scenes of contemporary life devoid of any anecdotal, historical, religious, or allegorical overtones. Often peopled by their family and friends, their landscapes were not the bucolic idylls of Barbizon but serene visions of picnicking, boating, reading quietly in a sunlit garden, or strolling along a road or deserted beach. And there was water nearly everywhere: the harbor at Le Havre, Argenteuil, or

Honfleur; the Seine at La Grenouillère; the rain-soaked boulevards of Paris. Monet, especially, was obsessed with the reflective properties of water.

More than anything else, however, the subject matter of Impressionist paintings was light itself—the shifting, glowing, vibrating effects of sunlight on a multitude of surfaces under various atmospheric conditions. These artists were not telling stories; they were capturing "impressions" of particular places at particular times. The Salon-going public was incapable of comprehending this totally original approach.

What they found even more difficult to come to terms with was the Impressionists' broken brushwork and intense color. The paintings in the Paris Salon were slick and smooth, glossy and perfect, with brushwork so refined as to be undetectable. They were, in a word, "finished." This was the academic ideal, and the Impressionists' obvious departure from it confused the public and incensed the critics. As Emile Cardon wrote in *La Presse* after seeing the 1874 exhibition, "...To render the impression without defining line, without color, without shadow or light...is quite simply the negation of the most elementary rules of drawing and painting." (Dunlop, *The Shock of the New*, p. 85).

The Impressionists' approach was unprecedented. In an effort to catch the momentary effects of light, they worked rapidly over all parts of the canvas at once. Pissarro once told a young painter how to do it: "Use small brush strokes and try to put down your perceptions immediately....Cover the canvas at the first go, then work at it until you see nothing more to add." Figures, landscape, sky, water—all were fused into a network of short, separate, comma-shaped strokes that flickered visibly over the picture's surface. This technique gave the completed work a sketchy quality that appeared *un*finished. Yet, as the poet Jules Laforgue wrote in one of the first insightful analyses of the new movement, it was precisely this break with hard-edged detail and meticulous brushwork that made the Impressionists' paintings fresh and new:

> In a landscape bathed in light, in which people are modeled like colored grisailles, where the academic painter sees only white light outspread, the Impressionist sees it bathing everything not with a dead whiteness, but with a thousand vibrant clashings, with rich prismatic decompositions. Where the academic sees only the outline binding the modeling, [the Impressionist] sees the real, living lines, not taking geometric form but built up with a thousand irregular touches which, from a distance, convey life. Where the academic sees things fitting into their regular respective planes according to a framework reducible to a pure theoretical diagram, [the Impressionist] sees perspective established through a thousand nuances of tone and touch, through the varied conditions of the air laid out not on a motionless but on a moving plane.
>
> (Blunden, *Impressionists and Impressionism*, p. 126.)

The bright colors on this moving plane caused, perhaps, the greatest sensation. The sight of "blue children" and faces blotched with "curds of intense violet" both horrified and amused the public. The Impressionists were the first to venture beyond the boundaries of traditional color, attempting to reproduce fragments of light in small, glowing patches. They frequently painted with unmixed, "pure" color, or they blended a desired shade directly on their canvases. This was made possible by the availability of oil paint in flexible zinc tubes, an innovation of the second half of the nineteenth century. Before then artists had to mix their own paints on a palette, using ground pigments and solvents, or buy them ready-mixed from a dealer. Either way there was wide variation in both quality and hue. Packaging oil paint in zinc tubes standardized colors and led to the introduction of new ones. As Renoir noted, this simple invention also gave the artist the freedom to work out-of-doors:

> Paint in tubes, being easy to carry, allowed us to work from Nature and Nature alone. Without paint in tubes there would have been no Cézanne or Monet, no Sisley or Pissarro, nothing of what the journalists call the "Impressionists." Thanks to modern chemistry the colors [still] have a vividness and richness which the old masters never dreamed of."
> (Blunden, *Impressionists and Impressionism*, p. 59.)

The Impressionists banished all earth tones, burnt sienna, and black from their palettes. Monet, who in later years grew weary of being asked about his range of colors, limited himself to "silver white, cadmium yellow, vermilion, dark madder, cobalt blue, emerald green, and that is all." Renoir chose a similar but slightly broader array, including silver white, chrome yellow, Naples yellow, ocher, raw sienna, vermilion, rose lake, Veronese green, viridian, cobalt blue, and ultramarine blue.

The Impressionists exploited the full potential of these pigments by placing small brush strokes of complementary colors side-by-side to heighten the intensity of each individual tone. Red next to green, or yellow beside violet, made each appear brighter. This device indicated that the artists were aware of the various color theories and treatises on optics published during the mid-nineteenth century. The first and possibly most influential of these was written by Michel-Eugène Chevreul, a chemist. As director of the Gobelins tapestry factory, he conducted experiments on the optical effects of weaving complementary colors next to each another. He reported his findings on the nature of chromatic contrasts in two books, the first published in 1839 and the second in 1864. These were widely read by people in a number of fields, including many nineteenth-century artists from Eugène Delacroix on.

While the Neo-Impressionists of the 1880s used Chevreul's conclusions as the basis of a specific formula for painting, the Impressionists appear to have applied them intuitively. In fact, a number of their ideas about color evolved not from reading books but from carefully observing nature. The more they worked in the open air, the more they realized that shadows, for example, were not black and colorless but contained reflected hues that were richer in value and generally bluer than their sunlit surroundings. This was especially apparent in shadows cast on snow, as Renoir explained to a young painter who had used too much white in painting a snowy landscape:

> White does not exist in nature. You admit that you have a sky above that snow. Your sky is blue. That blue must show up in the snow. In the morning there is green and yellow in the sky. These colors also must show up in the snow when you say that you painted your picture in the morning. Had you done it in the evening, red and yellow would have to appear in the snow. And look at the shadows. They are much too dark. . . . Shadows are not black; no shadow is black. It always has a color. Nature knows only colors. . . . White and black are not colors.
>
> (Rewald, *History of Impressionism*, p. 210.)

Colored shadows and the Impressionists' preference for unmixed colors meant that the entire tonality of a painting became brighter and more intense. The public of 1874 was so unaccustomed to seeing such vivid color, especially in the blue-indigo-violet range of the spectrum favored by these artists, that it perceived an all-pervasive blue-violet haze in Impressionist paintings that modern-day viewers no longer discern. This "indigomania," as J.K. Huysmans termed it, greatly disturbed both the public and the critics, some of whom seriously tried to discover some reasons for this "aberration" in the Impressionists' vision. One critic suggested that they saw "ultraviolet," explaining that when one looked too long at yellow in brilliant sunlight, this created a negative after-image of violet. Albert Wolff, an influential Parisian art critic and connoisseur, cited the violet tones as proof that the artists were all lunatics. Huysmans, later a proponent of the Impressionists, was also initially repulsed by their bright colors and violet-tinged atmosphere:

> I don't want to name names here, suffice it to say that the eye of most of them had turned monomaniacal; this one saw parrot blue in all of nature; that one saw violet; earth, sky, water, flesh, everything in his work was tinged with lilac and deep purple.
>
> (Quoted in Oscar Reutersvard, "Journalists (1876-1883) on 'Violettomania,'" *Impressionism in Perspective*, p. 39.)

He, too, attempted to find a scientific explanation for why the Impressionists saw so much blue and violet:

> Their retinas are diseased. The cases certified by the oculist Galezowski and cited by Veron concerning the atrophy of several nerve fibers of the eye and notably the loss of the notion of green, which is the warning

symptom of this type of ailment, were without a doubt like the cases of these painters. For green has almost disappeared from their palettes, whereas blue...persisting until the end in this disorder of sight, dominates and drowns everything in their canvases.

(Quoted in Oscar Reutersvard, "Journalists (1876-1883) on 'Violettomania,'" *Impressionism in Perspective*, p. 41.)

Later, of course, Huysmans and others became accustomed to the Impressionists' color and technique and grew to like their paintings. They attributed this change in attitude to the artists' return to a palette that was true to nature—following their "recovery" from their "retinal disorders"!

D espite the torrent of public scorn and critical sarcasm that greeted their first group exhibition in 1874, the Impressionists fervently believed in what they were doing. Encouraged only by one another and a coterie of loyal friends and patrons, they persevered. Because sales were few, the artists lived on credit and were almost constantly in debt. Monet, at a low ebb, once wrote: "Desperate state. I sold a still life and can work a bit. But as always I've stopped for lack of paint...." It was not only paint that he lacked; Renoir brought him bread so he would have enough to eat.

Virtually all of the Impressionists suffered through years of hardship. Their straitened circumstances were further complicated by their own expectations. The Bohemian lifestyle did not become popular until the next generation, toward the end of the century, when artists such as Paul Gauguin and Toulouse-Lautrec pioneered it; most of the Impressionists had middle-class backgrounds, and they felt obliged to maintain a respectable middle-class standard of living for themselves and their families. In the 1870s and 1880s, this meant not only supporting a wife and children but also providing them with nicely appointed living quarters, preferably outside of Paris; keeping one or more servants; and having the means to entertain friends with good food and wine. It cost money to have a studio in Paris, as many artists did, and to buy paint and canvas.

All of these obligations had to be met out of an unpredictable income. Most of the Impressionists had to rely on the patience of their creditors or trade paintings for food, rent, art materials, and other necessities. Any money generated by sales, which were infrequent, usually went toward paying off debts.

During these years of financial uncertainty, many of the artists counted on Paul Durand-Ruel to provide them with something resembling a steady income. Durand-Ruel was not only an early supporter of the Impressionists but also served as their principal dealer. He first met Monet and Pissarro in 1870 in London, where many artists had sought refuge from the Franco-Prussian War, and bought several of their paintings then. Back in Paris again, Monet and Pissarro introduced him to Renoir, Sisley, Degas, and Manet, and he began buying their works as well. A man with intuition and a good eye, Durand-Ruel was a friend and patron of the Impressionists at a time when few others appreciated them. He advanced them money and took their paintings even when he was not sure that he would ever sell them. Although he was on the verge of bankruptcy more than once during the 1870s, his gamble eventually paid off.

In early 1886 Durand-Ruel headed for New York with 300 canvases by painters including Monet, Renoir, Degas, Pissarro, Sisley, and Morisot. American artist Mary Cassatt, the daughter of a wealthy Pittsburgh banker and a close friend of Degas, Renoir, Monet, and others in the group, had helped to arrange a two-month-long exhibition that would serve as the American public's introduction to Impressionism. The critics were cautious, but the exhibition did not generate the outpouring of ridicule that had greeted the first Impressionist show in Paris a dozen years earlier. A number of paintings were quickly sold to important collectors, and the entire venture was such a success that Durand-Ruel repeated it the following year. "Without America," he later recalled, "I was lost, ruined, through having bought so many Monets and Renoirs. Two expositions there . . . saved me." Renoir agreed, stating: "We perhaps owe it to the Americans that we did not die of hunger."

By the mid-1890s American collectors and dealers were coming to France to buy directly from the artists, especially Monet. This signaled the beginning of prosperity and financial security for the Impressionists, most of whom were then in their fifties, for the Americans had money and were willing to pay whatever the artists asked. In this way, many of their finest paintings left France and were carried back to the States, where they later became the centerpieces of major museum collections.

It took longer for the French to develop an appreciation of Impressionism, and that they eventually came around was due to several factors. One was the growing importance of dealers such as Durand-Ruel and Georges Petit. Previously the annual Salon had been the chief marketplace for artists; private dealers gave them an alternative. If their works were rejected by the Salon jury, they had someplace else to take them. Once their fortunes were no longer tied solely to acceptance in the Salon, some artists stopped submitting to it altogether. Another factor was the appearance in the Salon itself of paintings by Renoir (from 1878 to 1883) and Monet (1880). The Impressionists had not yet entered into the mainstream of French art, but their vision—in certain canvases, at least—had become less offensive.

Impressionism remained controversial for quite some time, however, as was evident from the uproar over the Caillebotte Bequest in 1894. Gustave Caillebotte, an artist and a friend to many of the Impressionists, had inherited a fortune in 1873. Out of sincere admiration for his friends' works, combined with a desire to help them financially, Caillebotte began buying paintings by Monet, Renoir, Pissarro, Sisley, Degas, Manet, and Cézanne. His will, naming Renoir as executor, left his collection of sixty-five canvases to the State. There was one condition, however: the paintings would first have to be hung in the Luxembourg Museum and, ultimately, the Louvre.

      The government was scandalized. Negotiations over what, if anything, to accept dragged on for three years. The academic painter Jean-Léon Gérôme was passionate in expressing his indignation, and he was not alone: "I do not know these gentlemen and of the donation I know only the title. . . . Are there not some paintings of M. Monet in it? Of M. Pissarro and others? For the state to accept such filth would be a blot on morality." In the end, the State did take thirty-eight of the paintings; they now form the nucleus of France's Impressionist holdings.

      Rising prices were perhaps the surest indicator of the movement's growing popularity. Monet's works always fetched the highest prices, at least in the early years; at an auction at the Hôtel Drouot in 1875, for example, his paintings sold for between 180 and 325 francs, or about $175 to $300. By the turn of the century they averaged $2,000 to $3,000, with some going for considerably more. By 1926, when Monet died a rich man, the average price for one of his works was closer to $20,000, and today even his lesser works sell at auction for over a million dollars. Paintings by the other major Impressionists have experienced a similarly dramatic increase in value.

      Were Louis Leroy alive today he would, no doubt, be amazed. The paintings he thought suitable only for ridicule and sarcasm are among the most prized works of art in the world, and the names of their creators—Manet, Morisot, Monet, Renoir, Cézanne, Sisley, Pissarro, Degas—are among the most familiar in the history of art. It is his name that has been largely forgotten. When we do remember it, it is only because he coined the term that defined the movement he scorned.

THE DRAWINGS OF THE FRENCH IMPRESSIONISTS

Drawing is not what one sees, but what one must make others see.

— Edgar Degas

That drawing figured so prominently in the work of the French Impressionists was due in large part to the art schools of the time. When young artists chose painting as a career, it was assumed that they would first learn to draw. They next chose whether to follow Jean Auguste Dominique Ingres (1780-1867) or Eugène Delacroix (1798-1863)—in other words, classicism or romanticism.

The spirit of Ingres and his teaching methods, which were based on drawing antique statues or reliefs, drawing nudes, and composing historical scenes, still prevailed in the ateliers of the École des Beaux-Arts. Painting was taught to senior students only. Even then, the emphasis was on line rather than color, so much so that paintings actually resembled colored drawings. The ability to draw beautifully was highly valued, and many of the mistakes and shortcomings of academic paintings were excused if the works contained "noble contours."

Edgar Degas, more than any of the other Impressionists, was strongly influenced by Ingres, whom he knew personally. Ingres's work kept the traditional of classical drawing alive in France until the end of the nineteenth century, and many succeeding artists, including Henri de Toulouse-Lautrec (1864-1901), would be indebted to him.

In contrast, Claude Monet was not especially fond of Ingres, but even he could not escape the fact that a painter's education revolved around the techniques of drawing. When he visited Constant Troyon (1810-1865) in Paris in 1859, the animal painter advised him to draw as many nudes as possible because one could learn a lot from them. Monet's drawings, like those of Pierre Auguste Renoir, showed no sign of classicism. Charles Gleyre, who taught both Monet

11

and Renoir, once accused them of merely copying their model without keeping in mind the rules of classical art.

The Impressionists' immediate predecessors, the landscape painters of the Barbizon school, both acknowledged and rejected the importance of the drawing. While Théodore Rousseau (1812-1867) was a scrupulous draftsman, Diaz de la Peña (1807/8-1876) disapproved of the line and concentrated instead on color, which he applied in thick layers. And Camille Corot (1796-1875) advised Camille Pissarro to master two techniques, form and tonal value. These, he insisted, were the pillars of art; color and execution gave it its appeal.

D espite their schooling, the Impressionists saw color and light as more important than drawing. They were not interested in depicting reality in traditional ways, where the line was critical; in fact, they were not interested in depicting reality as a whole using any means. To them, light was all.

Toward the latter part of the 1880s, Edouard Manet and his friends used to meet in the Paris Café Guerbois (see reproduction I) to discuss problems of light and illumination. Manet believed that each object was made up of an illuminated part and a shaded part, and that shadow was best rendered by gradually adding gray. Monet, Renoir, Pissarro, and Alfred Sisley, all landscape painters, disagreed. They maintained that the shaded part was not completely devoid of light but instead contained a rich range of colors, mainly blue. By capturing these tones, they said, a painter could express depth without "grounding" the shaded part with the dark asphalt hues then in common use.

The landscape painters tried out their new ideas, primarily on winter motifs. When they painted shadows thrown on white snow, they included colors that complemented those that were evident in the illuminated areas. Monet and the other landscape painters took every opportunity to study the effects of color and light outdoors. For example, he and Renoir spent the summer of 1869 observing the way light reflected on water at La Grenouillère, a restaurant and bathing-place on the Seine at Croissy. Here they discovered that shadow was a combination of a motif's color, the color of the surroundings, and the color of the atmosphere itself. They began painting with subtle, light dots of color to better capture the movements of the water, the reflections of the light, and the shimmering of the air—what they considered to be the *real* landscape. They preferred to paint directly on white canvas without first sketching their subjects, but they did not entirely neglect drawing.

Only a few drawings have been handed down from this early Impressionist period; these are valuable for a number of reasons. They reveal the artists' efforts to apply to various motifs what they learned from painting out-of-doors. Each of the Impressionists developed relatively early a distinct artistic personality and style; these are often more obvious in the drawings than in the paintings. In addition, the drawings often disclose qualities that are not evident in the paintings, or they reveal and confirm what the paintings merely suggest.

Manet's pen-and-ink drawings, for example, indicate that he was an attentive observer, and his brush drawings evidence the quick-wittedness of an accomplished portraitist. Monet's early pastels surprise us with their almost expressive explosions of color, which also signal the painter's admiration for Delacroix; Renoir's pen-and-ink drawing of a female nude (plate 50) is reminiscent of Ingres. Alfred Sisley used colored chalks in much the same way he used oils to show vibrating air and light reflected on water.

The Impressionists' drawings also differed from one another technically, as we can see when we study Manet's ink washes, the pencil drawings of Degas, Berthe Morisot's watercolors, Monet's red chalk, pastel, or chalk drawings, Renoir's pure pen-and-ink drawings, Sisley's colored chalk drawings, Pissarro's gouaches, or Paul Cézanne's watercolors. But they all have at least two characteristics in common. One is the presence of light; the other is an appearance of "incompleteness," intended to convey an overall impression of the motif rather than a combination of details. These features are present in the paintings as well.

T he term "Impressionism," initially derisive, became the name of a movement which clearly differed from all other movements, both those which had preceded it and those which were contemporaneous with it. What made it unique was the fact that the artists did not choose their motifs—a nude, a still-life, a stand of trees, a village scene—for what they were, but rather for their colors and the way light affected them. What they painted and drew, how they painted and drew, and the techniques they used for painting and drawing all revolved around their desire to depict constantly changing natural light, and to express as naturally as possible the first impression evoked by the motif.

They cultivated their already heightened sensory perception during endless hours of painting out-of-doors. As a result of studying natural light and seeing the many colors in it, they gave up painting shadows in the traditional way. Their palette grew lighter, and color of a motif was often overcome by the colors of the surrounding atmosphere.

The painting technique they used—dots of rich, contrasting colors with no shading—offered several advantages. First, it enabled the artists to grasp more precisely the effects of light and its vibrations. Second, it allowed them to heighten the overall effect of colors by using them in their "pure" state. Third, it permitted them to capture rapid changes in the atmosphere, since it was faster than more conventional ways of painting. And finally, it resulted in motifs and objects merging into their surroundings.

This last point gave rise to a whole new understanding of drawing and its role in the picture. Pissarro, whose education included considerable amounts of theory, maintained that it was unnecessary to define a form by outlining it. Outlines were too hard. Instead, one could use dashes of color, and their shades and tonal values would in themselves produce outlines. Pissarro maintained that one of the greatest difficulties in painting lay not in getting the contours right but in shaping and depicting what was inside them.

Pissarro stated that an artist could paint however he or she wanted to, without being especially concerned about technique. After choosing a motif, however, one had to take into account everything to its right and left, everything above and below it. One had to paint over the entire canvas at once instead of concentrating on a single part at a time, and colors had to be balanced against their surroundings. The eye had to observe the subject as a whole, including the colors reflected in and on it, around it, and from it. When painting a landscape, for example, the artist had to be simultaneously aware of the sky, the water, the trees, and the ground, and gradually give form to all of these things until the final painting was identical to the original natural impression.

The Impressionists were not the first to recognize that outlines do not exist in nature; Eugène Delacroix had known this for quite some time. He was, in fact, a sort of indirect teacher to them. Manet visited Delacroix during his apprenticeship with Thomas Couture to ask Delacroix's permission to copy his *Dante and Vergil in Hell*. Degas combined his reverence for Ingres with an honest admiration for Delacroix; he had 56 of Delacroix's drawings in his personal collection. Monet and Frédéric Bazille, who lived together for a time, used to watch Delacroix at work from the window of their house; they were amazed to see that he let his models walk around while he was drawing them.

The Impressionists adopted Delacroix's belief that outlines were only imagined. Instead of lines, they used dashes of color. Traditional contours dissolved into their surroundings, and linear energy was replaced by the rhythm of these individual strokes and the picture's color structure.

It is a mistake to assume that the Impressionists always thought alike on everything, however. While Monet, Sisley, and Pissarro tended to adhere to similar principles, Manet and Degas initially objected to them. When they gradually came around, they arrived at a new synthesis of sensibility and freed color. Renoir and Cézanne actually turned away from Impressionism in later years, searching the classical past for support; they ultimately reached a point of originality and artistic representation that would have a profound influence on twentieth-century painting.

The eight artists who formed the core of the Impressionist group got together more or less by accident during the 1860s. But it was no accident that they were united by a common name for several years afterward, despite differences in birth, talent, education, and their understanding of art and its objectives and methods. Their main connection may have been their age: all were born between 1831 and 1841. Together they represented the "younger generation," in comparison to the realists from the 1820s. They also had similar experiences in the artistic circles of Paris, then dominated by academicism, and together they opposed the official art of the time.

Upon closer observation, we can distinguish three groups: the students of the Académie Suisse (Pissarro, Cézanne, and Armand Guillaumin); the students of Gleyre at the École des Beaux-Arts (Monet, Renoir, Sisley, and Bazille, who was later killed in the Franco-Prussian War); and the third group, composed of Manet and his friends Degas and Morisot (Manet and Degas both studied at the École des Beaux-Arts—Manet with Thomas Couture, Degas with Louis Lamot; Morisot studied with Camille Corot).

It was Monet who brought all three groups together. He had attended the Académie Suisse, where he met Pissarro, before entering Gleyre's atelier in 1862; he and Pissarro were introduced to Manet in 1866. When Manet met Morisot two years later, the group that would be known as the Impressionists was largely complete.

They started planning an exhibition of their own as early as 1867, seeking freedom from what they viewed as the obstinate doctrines and chicanery of the Paris Salon and its jury. Their plan was abandoned for a while due to lack of money, the intervention of the Franco-Prussian war, and the death of Bazille, but the idea lived on and surfaced again some six years later. The economic crisis of 1873 made it necessary for the art dealer Paul Durand-Ruel to stop patronizing them for a period of time, and it became clear that they would have to generate other means of support.

And so it was that the first exhibition of the *Société anonyme des artistes, peintres, sculpteurs, graveurs, etc.* (Anonymous Society of Artists, Painters, Sculptors, Engravers, etc.) opened on April 15, 1874—and inaugurated a new epoch in art and art history. This group of "anonymous" young painters would not only influence European painting and sculpture for decades to come, but would also have an impact on music, literature, and theater.

Edouard Manet

Although Pissarro (1831-1903) was the oldest member of the group, Manet (1832-1883) became its leading personality. His personality, his appearance, his social standing, and his reputation as an artist made him well suited for this role.

Manet came from an upper middle-class family. He wanted to be a painter, and he convinced his parents to let him try. He also wanted to be successful and esteemed by the public, so he chose as his teacher the then-famous Thomas Couture at the École des Beaux-Arts.

Manet studied with Couture for six years. When his teacher once said, "Manet, you will never be more than the Daumier of your day," he not only correctly identified the core of Manet's genius but also predicted the storm of protest that Manet's work would provoke in the very near future.

Manet first gained a name and an important position among his contemporaries at the early age of 28, when his *Spanish Guitar Player* was exhibited at the Paris Salon in 1860. His friends were impressed by the way the painting linked romanticism and realism and appreciated the fact that it convincingly "translated" the work of the great Spanish painters, Diego Velázquez (1599-1660) and Francisco de Goya (1746-1828), into a modern artistic language.

But when he showed his large composition, *Le Déjeuner sur l'Herbe*, in the Salon des Refusés in 1863, he caused a scandal that would be repeated two years later with the showing of *Olympia*. The critics and the public alike were shocked by these works, even though they dealt with classical themes and despite the fact that Manet was obviously referring to the great masters of the Renaissance.

These paintings were conceived in an entirely new way, without adherence to convention, and they established a new way of seeing. In them Manet both actualized the content—the Paris reality of the time appeared in undiminishedly keen liveliness—and gave priority to formal artistic viewpoints. The motif was not important; reflections on the relation between color and light took precedence. Manet's technique was also exciting. He worked with tonal values, but nobody else before him had ever achieved such powerful luminosity and brightness.

The other young painters greeted Manet's originality with enthusiasm and began perceiving him as their leader. He, however, was not interested in collaborating with the rebels and continued to pursue his objectives within the confines of more official institutions. He disliked being called an "Impressionist" and consequently refused to take part in their group exhibitions so as not to compromise himself before the Salon jury.

Still, one could not study the history of French Impressionism without taking his work into account. Although Manet does not rank among the avant-gardists or the founders of the new movement—Claude Monet deserves most of the credit for that—he contributed considerably, if indirectly, to its development. He was the creator of modern painting and the

I   Edouard Manet, *Paris Café* (probably the Café Guerbois), 1869

advocate of a progressive conception and awareness of life.

He once wrote in his diary that "to be a man of this time one must paint what one sees." With these words he branded himself an Impressionist. Similarly, J. K. Huysmans commented on his talent for capturing a passing moment and bathing it in light. In other words, Manet was doing what his friends were doing and could not help but be connected with them despite his protestations to the contrary.

He refused at first to accept the Impressionists' opinions on light and shadow. He continued to produce line drawings and to paint with blacks and grays, although he achieved the plastic-spatial effect through the flat application of color instead of shading. With this new technique, and due to the fact that he consciously painted modern life, Manet prepared the way for the Impressionists.

He drew throughout his life, as if drawing were an organic and inseparable part of his work; in his later years he combined it with color. His love

17

II   Edouard Manet, study for *Boating*
(also called *Boating at Argenteuil*), 1874

for drawing began during his early school years; he enhanced his abilities
in Couture's studio and by copying the old masters in the Louvre and other
important art galleries in Western Europe. In addition, he made written
notes of impressions from and occurrences in everyday life.

Many of Manet's drawings are now in the Louvre. About them, his friend
Antonin Proust wrote, "In these sketches, whether they copy old masters
or convey an immediate impression of nature, there is not one stroke that
would be unnecessary, no accent that would not fit. Everything is presented
with such a sureness of hand which reveals—next to the absolute will—
that passion for truth that formed the dominating trait of character of his
genius."

III Edouard Manet, *Portrait of*
Claude Monet, 1870s

IV Edouard Manet, *Portrait of*
Gustave Courbet, 1878

To quickly capture impressions of the moment, Manet used pencil, red chalk, or sepia. He marked out the form with an outline without rounding it off plasticly and used flat brush strokes to indicate light and shadow without modeling or changing tones. His line was broad and soft and accentuated the flat dash of color.

Following the example set by the old masters, he prepared all larger works by first doing several drawings and sketches from nature and then executing the entire composition in watercolor. After his journey to Spain in 1866, his watercolors showed a more relaxed style and achieved a certain independence from the final painting; he sometimes completed additional watercolors, free copies, after finishing a painting.

Most of his drawings retain the function and meaning of a sketch. They were meant to capture a vague impression, a quick movement, or a characteristic pose or gesture. He always kept drawing paper at hand and carried a sketchbook and pencil with him whenever he went for a walk. Even his vaguer sketches are evidence of the sureness with which he was able to capture and express the characteristic movements that help to form the overall expression of a work. In this respect he was similar to Hokusai, the Japanese master of the colored woodcut, who achieved perfection of characterization in his prints through the simplicity of his means of expression. Manet admired and delighted in Hokusai's work and considered it an example of how best to convey a subject's most typical traits while ignoring the insignificant aspects.

The reproductions in this volume include numerous observations of society—sketches and studies, pen-and-ink drawings, watercolors, and portraits in pastel. *Concert in the Tuileries* (plate 1), for example, demonstrates the perfection Manet achieved early in his career with wash over India ink. The watercolors *Spanish Dancers* and *Lola de Valence* (plates 2 and 3) are representative of his Spanish period; they also demonstrate how much Manet learned from Goya about the use of flat dashes of color. Manet employed this technique most successfully in his brush-and-Chinese-ink drawings, which included portraits of his friends Gustave Courbet (1819-1877) (reproduction IV) and Monet (reproduction III) and studies for paintings. The study for *Boating* (reproduction II) reveals the painter's enthusiastic pursuit of such Impressionistic problems as changing light and reflections in nature.

Among the drawings which Manet created to document the atmosphere of Paris in the latter half of the 1800s (see *Paris Café*, reproduction I, and *Rue Mosnier, Paris*, plate 14), *The Barricade* (plate 12) stands out as especially dramatic. It depicts an execution of the Communards, defenders of the Paris Commune, in 1871. The composition of the firing squad was taken almost exactly from Manet's painting, *The Execution of Emperor Maximilian of Mexico By A Firing Squad.*

The lovely *Portrait of Berthe Morisot* (plate 10)—one of the artist's most beautiful pencil drawings—may be viewed as a standard for Manet's skill at portraiture. The light watercolor *Irises* (plate 11), done with a touch of color, reveals the artist's fascination with flowers and his response to their overwhelming charm—and predicts the coming of Art Nouveau.

Manet painted his first important pastel in 1874 and used this medium almost exclusively during the last years of his life, when illness kept him bedridden and unable to work in oils. He was attracted to pastels both by their ease of use and their undisputed pictorial quality. With only a few strokes, he was able to indicate colored areas and to gradate tonal values without detracting from their uniqueness and character.

Manet found the complicated technical finesses of Degas unacceptable. He kept instead to the traditional eighteenth-century French pastel, adapting it to suit his own needs and artistic intentions. He mainly drew portraits of his friends— poets, painters, and writers; he also drew the poor people who visited him in his studio and liked to model for him. But he seemed particularly fascinated with the pretty and elegant women of Paris—the dancers, actresses, and ladies of high society. In these pastel portraits (see, for example, the model for *Bar in the Folies-Bergères*, plate 13), Manet went beyond drawing alone and surrendered to his passion for painting.

He sold only a few pastels, and at ridiculously low prices. Being a true gentleman, he gave most of them away to the women who posed for them, knowing they would be pleased with their gifts. Some of the personalities he portrayed are known to us: Madame Zola, Antoine Guillement, Méry Laurent, Mademoiselle Lemmonier, Marie Colombier, and Irma Brunner, called "The Viennese" (see plate 15); most others remain anonymous. Each portrait is a small gem in itself, shimmering in delicate shades of color.

Edgar Degas

Edgar Degas (1834-1917) resembled Manet in both character and appearance. A well-educated, witty, always well-dressed and entertaining son of a Paris banker and student of Louis Lamothe, he was considered the natural successor to Ingres. In 1855, when the then 21-year-old law student decided to become a painter, Ingres told him: "Draw lines, young man, many lines; from memory or from nature, and using a model; it is in this way that you will become a good artist." Degas remembered these words all his life.

He first became a student at the École des Beaux-Arts, after which he traveled to Italy to study and copy Renaissance art. For his first composition, in 1860, he chose a classical theme from Greek history. In 1865 he had a first showing in the Salon of conventional medieval war scenes.

The idea of becoming a painter of historical scenes bothered him. Soon, however, his skill as an observer and his interest in experienced reality became apparent despite the academic bent of his work. His interest in Italian painters grew to encompass not only those of the Renaissance but also the primitives. In addition to his compositions from classical history, he drew horses at the racetrack; he and Manet were a typical pair of dandies. At the same time he worked on psychologically fascinating portraits of his friends and acquaintances, and in 1867 began to seek out the worlds of music, opera, and especially ballet. A great admirer of Courbet, Degas gradually extended his range of realistic themes to include washerwomen at work, women ironing, and scenes from milliners' shops and cafés.

For a long time, Degas—whom Paul Valéry called "the world's most intelligent, deliberate, demanding, and stubborn graphic artist"—remained outside the Impressionist group and Manet's circle of friends. He enjoyed his solitude and was reluctant to reveal anything about his personal life. Unlike the Impressionists, he was not interested in painting out-of-doors, and he rarely painted landscapes. From the beginning he focused on the human figure.

Given the success he achieved with his early portraits of acquaintances from the Paris upper middle class, he could have become a painter of high society. But his sensitivity to life in all its forms eventually drove him to the rebellious Impressionists. While they devoted themselves to the problems of light, however, Degas searched for a line that would contain something of Jean-Antoine Houdon's (1741-1828) statues and Maurice Quentin de Latou's (1704-1888) pastels and possess a liveliness that would absorb everything elemental in nature.

The Impressionists consciously adapted their painting style to be able to truly capture the first impression; Degas, on the other hand, would not consider spontaneity, inspiration, or temperament. Neither did he think much of the observation of nature, a practice which the Impressionists swore by and were completely devoted to. He considered painting a conventional art, and drawing in the style of Holbein was more important to him than studying in the open air.

In 1872 Edgar Degas began attending rehearsals of the Paris Opera ballet. He discovered behind the scenes a world to which he would return again and again throughout his life. It did not require him to relinquish his strict attention to order. In the ballet he found the movement he had been looking for—neither free nor spontaneous but thought out and calculated. Ballet, like horse racing, was subject to strict discipline and rules. The combination of instinct and precision excited him.

Just as he was able to commit to memory every step a horse took and every expression it revealed, he was able to quickly capture the essence of a dancer. He drew hasty sketches in the theater or rehearsal room and painted them in detail in oil when he returned to his studio. Contrary to the Impressionists, who insisted on having their motif in front of them while painting, Degas believed that one could not paint while observing—and, conversely, that one could not observe while painting. But these convictions did not prevent him from keenly grasping the Paris of his day. He developed a catalogue of subjects to which, in the 1870s, he added concert, circus, and vaudeville scenes.

Simultaneously he searched for new ways of drawing, which he considered to be more versatile than painting. He drew the same subject over and over—ten times, a hundred times—and did not find this hard to do, since he held to the opinion that in art nothing should be left to chance, least of all movement. He reproached the Impressionists for becoming slaves to nature, light, and their insistence on capturing immediate impressions. According to Degas, it was proper to copy what one saw but preferable to draw from memory, since a recollection could only be improved by imagination. By putting imagination above copying he was able to deal freely with the details in his compositions. While the Impressionists had to complete their pictures over several sittings at the same location, Degas was able to change his at any time—and, as a result, improve and perfect them. He was never satisfied with his paintings, and he was reluctant to exhibit or sell them since this would have made it impossible to improve them.

Like Manet, Degas began working more with pastels starting in the 1870s. They brightened his palette and, unlike his oil painting, led him toward greater simplification. He was influenced by Japanese colored woodcuts, which the Impressionists had discovered and begun to collect. He also began dabbling in photography, which inspired him to bold foreshortenings and asymmetric compositions.

Portrait of Edouard Manet (plate 16) and *Manet at the Races* (plate 17) leave no doubt as to where the young artist derived his direction. The school of Ingres is especially apparent in the latter, drawn from life at the racetrack. A true portraitist, Degas was primarily interested in the face. *Dancer Adjusting Her Slipper* (plate 19) reveals much about the nature of the artist's study of dancers. Everything in the composition is aimed at finding the right moment in the movement—the silhouette—so that it gives the impression of an instantaneous picture, almost a photograph.

Beginning in 1880, when his eyesight was weakening, Degas freed his drawings of all nonessential elements and concentrated on primary subjects and features. He switched from soft pencil, black chalk, and gouache to fat chalk and charcoal to achieve complex and marked effects. He began working almost exclusively in pastels rather than oils, and brought new applications to that medium with inventive procedures and technical refinements unknown before then. Although many of his pastels seem like paintings because of their color character, drawing often—surprisingly—dominates. This is most apparent in the hatching he used to plasticly model faces in works including *After the Bath* (plate 22) and *Three Russian Dancers* (plate 24).

Other than dancers, women making their toilette became Degas's favorite subject during his late period. He completed several nude studies of women in different positions—bathing, washing, drying themselves off, combing their hair, looking in the mirror. He developed a new kind of nude, rejecting conventional poses and seeking instead natural, everyday gestures. He even had bathtubs and wash basins brought into his studio for works such as *After the Bath* and *Woman Bathing* (plates 22 and 23).

In his late pastels, Degas reduced the drawing even more and heightened the expressiveness of the color. Each line became a color accent with a function similar to that of the brush stroke in the oil paintings of the Impressionists. His ecstatically flaming shades were fireworks; form was dispersed in the bright texture of colored lines, as in *Dancers* (plate 26).

The work of Edgar Degas, the keen analyst and sharp observer of his time, came to a close with fantastic coloristic compositions in which the studies of absolute reality changed into overwhelming colored visions.

Berthe Morisot

The only woman who took part in the formation of the Impressionist group and remained true to it until the end was Berthe Morisot (1841-1895). Manet and Degas first met her in 1868, after she had been exhibiting her pictures regularly in the Paris Salon for over four years.

The daughter of wealthy, middle-class parents, Morisot began to study with Joseph Guichard, a disciple of Ingres and Delacroix, at the age of 16. When she was 18 she began accompanying her sister Edma to the Louvre to copy pictures. She admired the masters of the Barbizon school, in particular Camille Corot, who became her teacher two years later.

Morisot's distinct talent won immediate attention. When her painting, *View of Paris*, was shown in the Paris Salon in 1867, Manet was so taken by it that he wanted to paint a similar one right away. She met Manet and Degas in 1868, after she had been exhibiting in the Salon regularly for over four years. Then 27, she began modeling for Manet—she was the subject of *The Balcony*, for example—and she shared his admiration for the Spanish masters. In 1872 she took a brief educational trip to Toledo and Madrid, where she was particularly impressed by Goya.

V   Frédéric Bazille, *Self-Portrait*, late 1860s

Her works from this early period are reminiscent of Manet. But the influence was not one-sided; Manet's colors reflect her light palette.

At the first exhibition of the Impressionists in 1874, Morisot was represented by nine paintings, watercolors, and pastels. Renoir showed only six pictures; Pissarro and Sisley, five landscapes each; only Degas and Monet had more works on display than she.

Morisot soon began to favor watercolor and pastel techniques over oil and tempera painting. With them, the talented young painter was able to express most convincingly her unique conceptions and unusual hand.

In the December following the exhibition, she married Manet's younger brother Eugène and so became her friend's sister-in-law. She began associating closely with Monet, Renoir, and Sisley; together they organized an auction of their works in the Hôtel Drouot in 1875. She offered for sale pastels and watercolors as well as oils—and obtained the highest prices.

Morisot's early watercolors from the first half of the 1870s retain the charm of colored impressions. Delicate shades, thinned with water and consequently transparent, predominate. The artist used reflections on the white paper itself to increase the pictorial effect of these works, which were mainly family portraits and portraits of her friends, as in *Madame Gobillard and Her Daughter Paula* (plate 29).

When drawing with red or black chalk, Morisot paid equal attention to the subject's facial expression and clothing. With her line, broken in the Impressionist fashion, she was able to portray her models in a captivatingly lively way without ignoring psychological nuances; these are evident in such works as *The Artist's Daughter and Niece at the Piano* (plate 30).

Morisot took part in almost all of the Impressionist exhibitions, with the exception of the fourth one in 1879. After the final exhibition in 1886 she maintained her friendships with the other painters in the group and exhibited with them in the Petit Galerie. Both Renoir and the Neo-Impressionist Georges Seurat (1859-1891) highly praised her work. Seurat was especially taken with the charm and vivaciousness of her watercolors and the touching sincerity and sensitivity of her visions on canvas. Renoir was impressed by the maidenly characteristics of her art; after viewing her portraits of children and her depictions of maternal bliss, he termed her the last true painter of the French rococo.

Claude Monet

The most important personality of French Impressionism was probably Claude Monet (1840-1926). He was born in Paris but spent his childhood and youth on the rocky shore along the seacoast of Le Havre, where his father had a grocery store. By age 15 he was already earning pocket money drawing caricatures (see, for example, reproduction VI). Then the landscape painter Eugène Boudin (1824-1898) took him under his wing and taught him how to observe nature. Three of Monet's guiding principles can be traced back directly to him: First, that freshness and liveliness cannot be obtained in the studio; second, that the overall artistic impression is always more important than detail; and third, that the first impression must always be remembered and accurately expressed.

When he was 19, Monet traveled to Paris. There he was advised by the painter Constant Troyon, admired the work of Corot and Charles François Daubigny (1817-78), frequented the artists' cafés, and visited the famous Académie Suisse, a studio where a model was always available and the professors made no corrections. He also formed a friendship with Pissarro, and the two became so close that they drove to Champigny-sur-Marne together in April of 1860 to paint in the open air.

He served in the military in Algeria and returned with unforgettable impressions. Under the bright sunlight and vivid colors of the African sky, he had made rapid progress toward artistic maturity. Upon his return to Le Havre in 1862 he became friends with the Dutch landscape painter Johan Barthold Jongkind (1819-1891), who painted with him in the open air and completed his education as a landscape painter. Monet owed to him the development of his powers of observation, which were now directed exclusively at changing light and atmospheric conditions; he was also indebted to Jongkind for the technique he used to capture his impressions.

At his father's insistence, he went to Paris later that same year to study with Charles Gleyre. There he met Bazille, the son of a rich Montpellier family, who was studying medicine; Renoir, the son of a poor tailor, who was working to finance his studies; and Sisley, born in France of wealthy English parents. Having already completed his years of apprenticeship, Monet familiarized his new friends with the life of an artist in Paris as well as with his experiences in landscape painting.

When Gleyre closed his atelier, Monet and Bazille went to Chailly, a village at the edge of the Fontainebleau forest, to study nature and become acquainted with the Barbizon landscape painters who lived and worked nearby. Monet was especially impressed by Daubigny and Jean-François Millet (1814-1875).

Unlike the Barbizon masters who, with the exception of Daubigny, only made sketches in the open air, the young painters began following Monet's example, painting outside in front of the motif. This made their palette lighter, and they learned to capture changes in form and colors caused by changes in lighting and atmosphere.

Monet had begun his artistic career by filling sketchbooks with caricatures of his teachers, classmates, and Le Havre notables. Now he continued to draw just as diligently—boats at sea, human figures. *Barks on the Shore* (plate 32) is a realistic drawing with sensitively reproduced, modeling light; the charming *Portrait of Camille Doncieux* (plate 35) reveals his skills as a portraitist. (He married Doncieux in 1870.)

Like Manet, Monet also used drawings to prepare his pictures, and he considered the pastel just as attractive as the pencil. At the first Impressionist exhibition in 1874 he showed seven pastel sketches in addition to five oil paintings—including the famous *Impression: Sunrise.*

His pastels from the latter half of the 1870s not only reveal his wild artistic temperament; they also show more clearly than the oil paintings his strong links with tradition. One can discern a close relationship with Courbet's Realism, as well as links to romanticism. The painter's attention was drawn to and held by contrasting light and effect, as is evident in both *The Saint-Siméon Farm* (plate 33) and *Tree in Front of a Farm* (plate 34).

Monet and Renoir often painted together. In 1869 they went to Grenouillère; 1874 found them in Argenteuil, the small town on the Seine that was made famous by the Impressionists. Monet was using the technique which calls for putting dashes of color directly on white canvas, without first sketching, to bring out diffused sunlight and the influence of the atmosphere.

During these years—the heyday of Impressionism—independent drawing became almost insignificant. This explains why we have so few drawings of Monet from this period, and their scarcity makes them even more precious. Like his oil paintings, they serve as reliable witnesses to the intentions of the Impressionist landscape painters. In *View of Rouen* (plate 36), for example, Monet succeeded brilliantly in capturing the flow of the Seine, its surface rippled by the wind, and the glimmering reflection of the river bank. He recorded these various elements with a style that ranged from thin lines in the sky to broad, dark shadows on the water.

In order to more closely observe reflections on water, Monet built a boat—as Daubigny, Renoir, and Sisley had done—and went down the Seine to Rouen. Gustave Caillebotte, a well-to-do engineer and naval expert, helped him build it; Caillabotte was also a painter and a supporter of the Impressionists, with whom he exhibited five times.

Monet participated in the first four Impressionist exhibitions in 1874,

VI Claude Monet, *Caricature of M. Ochard*, 1856-58

1876, 1877, and 1879. Yet when he sent works to be shown at the official Paris salon in 1880, Degas and the other members of the group considered him a turncoat. On the occasion of his one-man exhibition in Paris during that same year, however, he solemnly declared that he had never stopped feeling like an Impressionist and planned to remain one in the future. The seventh and next-to-last Impressionist exhibition in 1882 featured all of the old group except for Degas, and Monet met with his friends there; at the final exhibition in 1886, Monet, Renoir, and Sisley were missing.

Angler at the Seine near Pontoise (plate 38) is a classical example of the Impressionist art of drawing. Its long black-chalk lines, sensitively gradated with respect to thickness, create a perfect illusion of the river's reflecting surface. This is a typical Monet composition: the landscape, *sans* the sky, has been captured as a cutout seen from a moderate bird's-eye view, and the water fills the drawing, adding still more to the illusion.

Manet's death in 1883 signaled the end of an era for the group of artists who, despite misunderstandings and disagreements, had always managed to join forces for the public eye. They separated and everyone went his or her own way. Like the others, Monet underwent a crisis during which he destroyed several of his works and painted over others. More than anything else, however, he suffered from the feeling that art was no longer easy for him. His old creative enthusiasm did not return until he was staying in Giverny with his second wife, Madame Hoschedé.

In the artist's mind, Impressionism reached its peak in his series of haystacks, poplar trees, the cathedral of Rouen, and water-lilies from the 1890s. Realizing that light, which constantly changes over the course of a day, also alters one's perception of nature, he endeavored to catch the momentary impression as quickly as possible. Following each change, he stopped working on one canvas and tried to transfer the newly developed situation onto the next. With this almost scientific approach, he carried through the "law" of Impressionism—but he also lost his original spontaneity. After seeing these works, his Impressionist friends accused him of being rather ornamental.

Monet's drawings from this period attest to the artistic sovereignty of a painter who had just passed the fiftieth year of his life. His chalk drawing *Haystacks At Sunset* (plate 39), for example, gives the impression that sunlight, with its subtle reflections and tonal scale, is the only content. The soft, unrestricted structure, in which objects and forms melt and outlines are reduced to miniscule points, is characteristic of the Impressionistic hand.

Auguste Renoir

Pierre Auguste Renoir (1841-1919) and Monet were close not only in age—Renoir was the younger of the two by a scant four months—but also in the circumstances of their birth. Both came from poor families and had to earn their livings.

They shared other characteristics as well. Both had similar artistic dispositions; both had a gift for perceiving and reproducing reality.

VII   Auguste Renoir, *The Judgment of Paris*, 1908

Unlike Monet, however, who received a formal education in landscape painting while still a boy, Renoir had already led an eventful life when he entered Gleyre's studio. A trained porcelain painter, Renoir supported himself by decorating fans and curtains. This familiarized him with French rococo painting, the sensuality of which struck a responsive chord within him.

Monet was self-confident and determined; he always knew what he wanted and possessed a strong will. Renoir, on the other hand, was self-conscious, often vacillated between two extremes, and usually had to try several possibilities before making up his mind. Despite his poverty he was light-hearted and cheerful and gave the appearance of being a happy man—as long as he was painting. Since he had learned painting as a trade, he could work quickly and almost effortlessly.

Before Renoir began to work closely with Monet in 1869, Sisley was one of his best friends. In 1865 they painted together in Marlotte, a village near Barbizon in the Fontainebleau forest, and from there took a boat trip down the Seine to Le Havre, following Daubigny's example. During their trip they painted landscapes and studied light reflections on the water. They then returned to Marlotte, where Monet and Pissarro visited them and Renoir finally became acquainted with the work of Gustave Courbet.

In the summer of 1867, when Renoir painted his first picture outdoors, Courbet's influence gave way to the play of shadows which lent the composition a unique and peculiar charm. A beautiful pen-and-ink sketch for this work, *Lise with a Sunshade* (plate 42), not only represents Renoir's detailed preparation for the painting but also stands alone as an exemplary Impressionist drawing. The contour has been replaced by short parallel and sometimes crossing strokes that capture and reflect the light. As is the case in Impressionist painting, form has become a function of light.

When Renoir accompanied Sisley to Chailly, Sisley concentrated exclusively on landscape painting while Renoir was attracted by people. He especially liked portraying his friends—Sisley and his wife; Monet at work; Monet's wife, Camille.

Throughout his life, Renoir was obsessed by painting. In the studio, while taking a walk, or during his travels (which he relished), he always had a sketchbook at hand, and he filled it with all kinds of drawings. Many of these he destroyed, and others were later lost.

In addition to oil paintings, he showed one pastel at the first Impressionist exhibition in 1874. In 1879 a show consisting solely of his pastels was held in the gallery of the Paris publishing company of Georges Charpentier. Initiated by his brother Edmond, this was Renoir's first independent exhibition in that city.

Like Monet, Renoir suffered from existential difficulties. He was able to sell something once in a while simply because he painted portraits and nudes as well as landscapes. His pictures radiated a strange magic that affected even those viewers who otherwise rejected Impressionism out of hand. With the money from his infrequent sales, he was able to rent a small house with a garden in Montmartre and continue to paint in the open air. His famous painting, *Dancing at the Moulin de la Galette*, for which his painter friends and assorted beautiful women modeled, is a cheerful interplay between colored reflections, tonal values, and partial shadows on young faces under green treetops—an ode to oscillating light. Fascinated by dance motifs, Renoir returned to this subject several times.

As a result of a brief period of prosperity during which the art dealer Paul Durand-Ruel was buying pictures from Impressionists, Renoir was able to travel to Algeria and Italy in 1881. There he admired the frescoes of Pompeii and the works of Bonifazio de' Pitati (1487-1553) and Giovanni Battista Tiepolo (1696-1770). But it was the art of Raphael, which he saw in Rome, that made the strongest impression on him. He felt it to be "full of knowledge and wisdom... most beautiful in its greatness and simplicity." What he appreciated most about Raphael's frescoes was the fact that they were completely illuminated by sunlight although their creator had never worked in the open air.

Perpetually dissatisfied with his work, Renoir began to wonder whether he was neglecting drawing. During a personal crisis that occurred upon his return from Italy in 1883—he destroyed several pictures at that time—it turned out to be drawing that saved him. Depressed by the conviction that Impressionism had exhausted all its possibilities, and believing that he could not longer work in that fashion, Renoir turned to the old masters. He painted in the studio again instead of out-of-doors and continued the tradition of eighteenth-century painting. He began to despise the entire nineteenth century, dismissing it as an epoch when nobody could produce even a piece of furniture or a clock without imitating the past.

One result of his search for a way out of this dilemma were his pictures of bathers, female nudes, and dancing couples; Suzanne Valadon, the artist's brother Edmond, and the painter Paul Lhote modeled for some of the latter. Prior to beginning his two large pictures of dancers, Renoir made drawings that prepared the final composition in nearly every detail. *Dancing Couple* (plate 45), the pen-and-ink drawing for *The Dance at Bougival*, shows how drawing had refined Renoir's Impressionist hand without repressing any of its liveliness or ease. Light and its reflections are made more distinct in the drawing, by means of broken strokes and parallel hatching, than they ultimately are in the painting.

Women with Umbrellas (plate 43) is a study for the painting *The Umbrellas*. When we compare the two, we see that the former preserved the immediacy of the first impression while simultaneously conveying the sensual tenderness, color, and manner so typical of Renoir. This type of study demonstrates the perpetual charm of Renoir's work—which eventually won the favor of a public otherwise opposed to Impressionism.

After exhibiting his large composition *The Bathers*, for which he had been preparing for three years with pencil and red chalk (see *Three Bathers*, plate 46, and *Nude*, plate 47), in Petit's gallery in Paris in 1887, his Impressionist friends scolded him for disregarding the color tones of the picture in favor of the drawing. Renoir, however, was satisfied, for he had discovered a light and sensitive technique, close to the French rococo but new enough to warrant further development.

He had accomplished this by focusing all of his interest and attention on color. When he wanted red to stand out like a flag, he kept applying red and other colors until he had what he wanted. Just as Degas used pastels, Renoir used the red chalk technique, which he had adapted from François Boucher (1703-1770) and Jean Honoré Fragonard (1732-1806), to express his sensibility (see, for example, *The Judgment of Paris*, reproduction VII).

Even when he was a very old man, so weak that he could no longer hold the chalk or the brush in his hand, he fastened them around his wrist and kept working. Illness may have slowed him down, but it never detracted from his creative enthusiasm, his will, and his desire to paint and draw.

The range of bright colors in Renoir's late period was not intended merely to capture atmosphere and light. Instead, he used them to create an intensive, almost supernatural picture of life. In a very peculiar way that set him apart from Manet and Degas, Renoir brought out the velvet effect of pastels. He always worked with free color spots in predominantly warm tones—reds, browns, pinks, yellows—and contrasted them with small, pale-blue areas, rubbing some parts to achieve delicate transitions and using the white areas of the paper as a mirror (see *Bathing*, plate 53).

His watercolors from the vicinity of Paris (see *The Bridge at Argenteuil*, plate 51) and from Provence revealed his enormous enthusiasm for nature that symbolized, to him, paradise regained. In these, his personal artistic vision takes precedence over reality and is joined to his conviction that art is indescribable and inimitable.

Alfred Sisley

At the time Alfred Sisley (1839-1899) left Charles Gleyre's studio, he was fascinated by Corot's landscapes. He adored the way Corot depicted light—covering the landscape with a transparent veil, softening contrasts, diffusing sharp details, simplifying lines and areas. Even when he was painting with Renoir in Marlotte, Sisley remained true to Corot's example.

Sisley exhibited for the first time in 1866, showing two of his landscapes in the Paris Salon. After that, one or two of his pictures appeared there every other year until 1870. From 1871 to 1872 he resided in London, where he met the art dealer Paul Durand-Ruel. Upon his return to France he retired to Louveciennes and creative solitude. Inspired now by Monet, he searched for a new way of directly expressing nature. He studied the changing light and colors of the different seasons and strove to grasp the atmosphere of the landscape.

Like Corot, Sisley was a born poet. In Louveciennes, however, his landscape painting, which had been full of poetry, became bolder and more sure, radiating the same joy at the discovery of a newly-perceived reality that characterized the drawings and pictures of his Impressionist friends.

While in Gleyre's studio, the humble and sensible Sisley always remained in the background, especially in comparison to Monet and Renoir; while living and working with Renoir he bubbled over with gaiety, wit, and imagination. In a large group, his innate shyness prevented him from calling attention to himself and his opinions.

The Ferryman (plate 59) has all the characteristics of early Impressionism: a lyrical mood, a transparent atmosphere, bright shadows, and tender coloring. Corot's influence on Sisley is very noticeable here. The fine shades of the pastels work together with the paper, and the result is a deep space filled with sunshine. With its blurred background and detailed foreground, this drawing is similar to oil paintings of the time. Sisley succeeded in rendering light and shimmering air while simultaneously arousing the feeling that nature is one entity.

After the first Impressionist exhibition in 1874, Sisley traveled to England for a brief period. When he returned to France he again devoted

VIII   Alfred Sisley, *Farmers at Work*, c. 1894

IX   Alfred Sisley, *The Lumbermill*, 1877

himself to the landscape of Louveciennes, and after 1876 turned his attention to Moret-sur-Loing. Following Renoir's example, he sent pictures to the official Salon, but none of them was accepted. He did not even participate in subsequent Impressionist exhibitions—with the exception of the seventh and next-to-last one in 1882, where he showed 27 landscape paintings. Like Monet, Sisley did not draw very much, preferring instead to apply his oils directly to the canvas without first sketching. The sketches he did complete in the 1880s demonstrate the freedom of his graphic expression (see *La Canal du Loing*, plate 58, and *Le Canal de Bristol*, plate 56). Using only a few strokes, he was able to capture the terrain, the canal, small houses and trees on the banks, and human figures while preserving the mood of the landscape. These hastily executed drawings done in the open air seem to have been completed within a single breath; yet, perhaps for this reason, they make an impression of irresistible intensity. Sisley had a knack for penetrating the essence of nature with a few quick strokes and outlines.

He spent the last decades of his life in Moret. Long years of hardship and insecurity had made him suspicious, and he seldom got together anymore with his painter friends. He was troubled physically and emotionally after developing a temporary facial paralysis as an aftereffect of a cold. His dissatisfaction with himself grew as he got older, and he felt increasingly unhappy, tired, and disappointed with life.

Although he strove to imbue his work with a stronger and more passionate expressiveness, Sisley was at his best when guided by poetic intuition and the sensibility of his sight. He died, relatively unknown, in January of 1899; by 1900 the prices for his pictures had already begun to rise.

Camille Pissarro

Camille Pissarro (1830-1903), the son of a Creole mother and a Portuguese-Jewish merchant father, was born in St. Thomas in the West Indies. Like many other artists who would one day be known as Impressionists, he admired Camille Corot, whose works he first saw when he moved to Paris in 1855 to study painting. Like Corot, he had a poetic sensibility and yearned for perfection and harmony.

Determined to learn everything there was to know about painting, Pissarro moved from one studio to another at the École des Beaux-Arts and frequented the Paris cafés where the progressive painters, poets, and critics gathered. In 1859 he exhibited landscape paintings for the first time, in the Paris Salon. During that same year he met Monet at the Académie Suisse; two years later he became acquainted with Cézanne and Armand Guillaumin (1841-1927). In 1863 several of his pictures were shown at the Salon des Refusés.

He remained under Corot's influence until 1866, meeting with him often and taking his advice. He then found someone new to emulate—Courbet—and, like Renoir and Cézanne, parted ways with Corot when Corot

X   Camille Pissarro, *The Sower*, 1860s

did not support his new artistic intentions. His early drawings seem to reflect a variety of influences, including not only touches of Corot but also the Realism of Courbet and Millet. A strong expressiveness bordering on obstinacy in some of his figure studies (see, for example, *The Sower*, reproduction X) is also reminiscent of Vincent van Gogh (1853-1890).

In 1869 Pissarro moved to Louveciennes with his family. In 1870, when the Franco-Prussian War broke out, he fled to London; in his absence his house was occupied and all the works he had left behind were destroyed. In London he met Monet, and the two of them studied the English landscape artists for clues as to how to paint the London fog as well as winter and spring motifs.

The poetic winter atmosphere of *The Church on Westow Hill* (plate 65) has not lost any of its charm with age. In this watercolor a weak, cold sunlight shines through heavily laden snow clouds, the sky and the landscape

XI Camille Pissarro, *Harvesting Potatoes*, 1860s

have become one, and all contours merge into one another. White brush strokes like icy needles form tenuous accents in the colored fog.

Upon his return to France he settled in Pontoise. Meanwhile Paul Durand-Ruel had begun selling some of his pictures, along with those of Monet and Sisley. His artist friends often stopped by to solicit advice and support. Cézanne and his family lived nearby, and Guillaumin paid occasional visits.

As Monet and Renoir had done in Argenteuil, Pissarro and Cézanne worked side-by-side in the open air of Pontoise and painted the same motifs. During this phase Pissarro's expression gained sureness without losing any of its poetic content. His formerly dark coloring began to lighten. His friends admired both his distinct hand, which gave his pictures their definite character, and his ability to convey a deep, inner perception of nature. Only Paul Cézanne matched the degree of humility with which Pissarro approached nature to discover its hidden secrets.

Pissarro produced an important, extensive, and diverse pictorial and graphic oeuvre. Among the drawings of all the Impressionists, his show the greatest variety and complexity of technique, content, and artistic form. He applied

XII   Camille Pissarro, *Grazing in the Woods*, 1870s

a broad range of technical procedures and media, moving from pencil or pen over charcoal and brush to pastels, watercolor, and gouache; he also did etchings and lithographs. His drawings range from austere, realistic figure studies to purely Impressionistic watercolors, from psychologically penetrating portraits to illustrations and scenes taken from life.

Pissarro would probably be considered the "truest" Impressionist were it not for the fact that he switched to Neo-Impressionism in 1886; he was the only member of the group to do so. He was also the only one who participated in all eight Impressionist exhibitions, and none of his friends worked harder than he to propagate Impressionist ideas and methods. In comparison to the works of Monet, Renoir, or Sisley, which represented Impressionism's lyrical extreme, Pissarro's pictures are more earthy, robust, and realistic, and their coloring is more dense and material. Even when he was primarily concerned with light and its effects, he never forgot the plasticity of the form.

In 1882, following the second-to-last Impressionist exhibition, Pissarro experienced an artistic crisis. A long time passed before he was able to find his way out of it. The turning point came in 1885, when he met Seurat and Paul Signac (1863-1935) in Paris. He saw in their example a new, rational way to control his artistic instincts and was especially influenced by Seurat's theories of Optical Mixture, which maintained that secondary colors could be obtained by intermingling, rather than actually mixing, primary colors. This technique resulted in the colors "mixing" in the spectator's eye at a certain distance from the picture.

Pissarro began differentiating between "romantic" and "scientific" Impressions—to the dismay of his old friends, who could not accept his change in direction. Doubtless they were relieved three years later, in 1888, when Pissarro declared that the Optical Mixture method "inhibits me and hinders the development of spontaneity of sensation." He turned away from Neo-Impressionism and back to Impressionism again. His pictures regained their previous sensual freshness and received both attention and esteem, although they were never quite as successful as those of Monet or Renoir.

Pissarro's drawings retained ties to Realism through the 1880s (see, for example, *Sitting Peasant Woman*, plate 67, *Crouching Peasant Woman*, plate 68, and the study for *The Cat*, plate 69). In the watercolors from this period we find dashes of pure color juxtaposed in both direct impressions (see *Funeral of Cardinal Bonnechose*, plate 66) and psychological studies (see *Portrait of the Artist's Son Rudolph*, plate 71).

At the age of 50, white-haired and bearded, he looked like the biblical Abraham. Perpetually good-natured and warm-hearted, he was one of the most popular Impressionists. He knew how to teach with tact and without affectation; Berthe Morisot once said that "he could even teach rocks how to draw." It was Pissarro who first introduced Cézanne and Paul Gauguin (1848-1903) into the Impressionist exhibitions and familiarized them with Impressionist techniques

His *Self-Portrait* from 1888 (plate 73) depicts the 58-year-old artist as a wise old man who gazes at the observer with a profound, inquisitive expression. Here Pissarro demonstrated a variety of drawing techniques, from fine lines over vigorous hatching to thick, expressive strokes rendered with a reed pen.

Paul Cézanne

Paul Cézanne (1839-1906), the son of a banker from Aix-en-Provence, was supposed to study law, but what he really wanted was to become a painter, so he attended law school and drawing school at the same time. He and his classmate Émile Zola, the future novelist and critic, were inseparable companions and partners in numerous adventures.

Zola moved to Paris in 1858, and Cézanne spent two years fighting with his father for permission to go there and devote himself to art. Finally the elder Cézanne relented, and the son arrived there in 1861.

He enrolled at the Académie Suisse, where he became friends with Pissarro and Guillaumin and diligently prepared for the entry examination at the École des Beaux-Arts. When his hope for quick success faded, he returned to Aix-en-Provence and worked in his father's bank. But he was back in Paris again by November of 1862. He had won from his father the guarantee of a small allowance, and he never again gave up painting.

He took—and failed—the exam at the École des Beaux-Arts. He began submitting pictures to the Paris Salon in 1864, and all were rejected despite the intervention of Charles-François Daubigny, who became a member of the Salon's jury in 1866.

Emotionally volatile and wildly imaginative, Cézanne manifested his uncontrolled temperament in his eccentric and sometimes crude behavior as well as in his art. His peculiar paintings and slightly ponderous drawings were ridiculed by nearly everyone who saw them. Only Pissarro, who became his friend, recognized from the beginning that this difficult young man possessed a prodigious talent, and he sought to develop it further by encouraging Cézanne and working closely with him. While both admired Courbet, Cézanne sought to connect the older man's blunt, heavy Realism with his own preference for Spanish painting, in particular the dramatic works of Francisco de Zurbarán.

Although Cézanne had decided in 1866 to paint only in the open air, in truth he worked mainly in the studio. He preferred dark colors and an impasto technique—applying pigments thickly, layer by layer, with the brush or palette knife—and despite the obvious influence of Delacroix, Honoré Daumier (1808-1879), Courbet, and Manet, his works radiated a strange, almost brutal power that set them apart from all others.

Portrait of Achille Emperaire (plate 78) stands as one of the most beautiful drawings of his early period. Although somewhat derivative of Daumier, it reveals Cézanne's interest in forming the plasticity of the head and modeling the face as if he were sculpting rather than drawing.

In 1872 he went to Pontoise at Pissarro's invitation, and the two of them painted together in the open air. During this time Cézanne acquired the technique of juxtaposing small dashes of color, he replaced the light modeling of the form with the precise representation of tonal values, and he lightened and brightened his palette. His landscapes gained a new and unique expressiveness. Meanwhile, much to Pissarro's relief, he started keeping his temper in check.

In early 1873 he set out for Auvers to the home of Dr. Paul Gachet, where he painted a number of still-lifes and landscapes. His former laxity was replaced by a striving for accurate observation. Determined to capture the finest nuances, he patiently applied thick layers of paint, one on top of the other. His perceptions were so intense, and his desire to fathom the mysteries of nature and express them properly was so genuine, that the completed picture always gave the impression of freshness and immediacy despite the hours of work he put into it.

All his life, Cézanne both painted and drew, feeling that the two were intimately related. He tried to have them balance and complement each other. At one point he told his friend, Émile Bernard (1868-1941), that "drawing and color are by no means two different things. As you paint, you draw...the more harmonious the color, the more exact the drawing. The widest variety of colors can also attain a perfection of form." *Still Life with Fruit* (plate 76) evidences his ability to unite color and drawing. Pencil lines depict the plate and the forms of the different fruits lightly, but with a pronounced dynamic flourish; the watercolor shades—light orange, red, green, and violet—hint at the colors of each object.

Cézanne left several sketchbooks and a number of drawings on loose pages. Most were preliminary works for his paintings, and some were studies of the old masters. Drawings after Jacopo Tintoretto (1518-1594), Sir Peter Paul Rubens (1577-1640), Bonifazio Veronese, Gaspard Poussin (1615-1675), and Corot belong to this latter group. Unlike Degas and Renoir, Cézanne never concerned himself with sculpture, but he did draw the statues of Donatello (c. 1386-1466), Michelangelo (1475-1564), and his countrymen Augustin Pajou (1730-1809) and Pierre Puget (1620-1694). Some of these drawings surprise us with their unusual plastic energy (see, for example, *Study of Puget's "Hercules,"* plate 87).

Following the first Impressionist exhibition, Cézanne lived alternately in Paris and his home in Provence. In 1875 he and Guillaumin painted landscapes together on the banks of the Seine; in 1877 he and Pissarro worked side-by-side in Pontoise.

Meanwhile his desire for independence grew. He wanted to free himself from Paris and settle in the south, away from the noise of the city; at the same time, he wanted to "make of Impressionism something solid and durable, like the art of the museums." He refused to take part in the second Impressionist exhibition in 1876 but sent 16 pictures, primarily still-lifes and landscape paintings, to the third show in 1877. After that year he was rarely seen in Paris.

XIII   Paul Cézanne, *Camille Pissarro Searching for a Motif*, c. 1874

41

Cézanne gradually became a legend in his own time. He deliberately embellished his already notorious reputation with further provocative behavior. He spent the spring through the fall of 1881 with Pissarro and Gauguin in Pontoise; 1882 saw him in L'Estaque with Renoir.

Due to the influence of Antoine Guillemet, his former classmate at the Académie Suisse who became a member of the Paris Salon jury, Cézanne was finally allowed to exhibit there in 1882. This turned out to be an exception, for in subsequent years his submissions were rejected as usual. Since he did not participate in any of the Impressionist exhibitions after 1877, about the only place in Paris where one could see his works was the shop of the elderly color grinder M. Julien Tanguy, known as *père* Tanguy, and young painters went there to view them starting in the 1880s.

Cézanne's interest in plasticity, most evident in his drawings of statues, also found expression in his portraits. He modeled the head of his *Self-Portrait* (plate 79) much as if he were sculpting it, hatching where appropriate and carefully defining the form with soft lines. Only in difficult parts like the nose, the ear, and the eyes does the line become notably strong. In *Portrait of Madame Cézanne* (plate 80) the thicket of lines forms a shadow out of which the form bulges. The strong contrast between the tapered lines in the face and the dense, dark lines of the shadow are typical of the drawings from this transitional period.

Cézanne eventually rejected Impressionism, which he considered too superficial, but he preserved his highly developed color sense. He began focusing on spatial relationships and reduced form to its basic elements. Instead of using light to compose the form, he modulated color while retaining its transparency.

Balance, simplicity, and the significance of the form—those were the characteristics that young artists admired most in his pictures. In Cézanne's work they also found the solution to a problem they had been having: how to intensify emotion while simultaneously replacing empiricism with rational thought. They understood Cézanne's intent to achieve harmony between modern sensitivity and classical tradition; or, as he himself put it, "to vivify Poussin in contact with nature."

In his late drawings Cézanne continued to search for the nature of the form, largely by using parallel lines. However, a certain deformation of form soon became evident as the result of the contradiction between the form of the motif and the growing dominance of the composition. The study *The Tree* (plate 85) made it quite clear in which direction the painter's interest was turning. Here Cézanne demonstrated how an object could be confined to its basic structure, or form, and the space immediately surrounding it. Only the trunk and the branches are apparent; the roots are missing and the foliage is merely suggested. Disparate lines, setting the basic forms within the spatial plan, reveal something new about the essence of nature.

In 1895 the art dealer Ambroise Vollard organized an extensive Cézanne exhibition in Paris. His first big show, it was a revelation not only to the younger generation but also to his contemporaries, who finally acknowledged that the moody, difficult, irascible man was a superb painter.

The prices for his pictures began to rise. But the official recognition he yearned for all his life—shows at the Paris Salon, the ribbon of the Legion of Honor—continued to elude him. Two years before he died, he passed on his ideas about art to Émile Bernard.

Interestingly, it was the Cubists who carried forth his theories after his death. They attended the major retrospective of his works held in Paris in 1907 and came away enthusiastic about what they had seen.

The young artists who attended that exhibition were especially interested in the watercolors. Cézanne had considered them merely sketches for paintings; now they attained independent value.

A popular motif during his late period was Mount Sainte-Victoire, which towered above his home town. In *The Black Castle and Mount Sainte-Victoire* (plate 86), the content is lyrical, the expression economical, and the colors luminous. These characteristics, present in many of his watercolors, would have a profound effect on the development of twentieth-century painting.

The Impressionist movement was of relatively short duration. It began in the 1860s in the Salon des Refusés and in Charles Gleyre's studio at the Académie Suisse. It gained momentum in the Fontainebleau forest, in Paris cafés, and on the banks of the Seine. It had its public debut in 1874, at the first Impressionist exhibition; by the time of the last exhibition, in 1886, the original Impressionists were in the minority.

A few years earlier some of them had broken off from the group to search for new means of expression. At around the same time, another generation of artists had appeared on the scene: the Neo-Impressionists Georges Seurat and Paul Signac, the Symbolists Odilon Redon (1840-1916) and Paul Gauguin, the Expressionist Vincent van Gogh. They continued the tradition of resisting academicism, and followed the Impressionists' lead in much the same way the Impressionists had followed that of the artists of the Barbizon school.

Most of the Barbizon painters did not at first recognize the Impressionists as their legitimate successors (and some never did); nor did the Impressionists recognize the generation that came after them. Cézanne considered van Gogh to be a fool; Degas did not like Lautrec; Renoir, Monet, and Pissarro refused to acknowledge Gauguin's works from Tahiti. Meanwhile Gauguin accused the Impressionists of simply painting what they saw and ignoring what exists in the mysterious inner recesses of the mind.

Impressionism represented—at least initially—a joint effort by artists who influenced and supported one another in the search for a new way of expression that would grant each of them an individual creative language. Once they had succeeded, they parted, and each went his or her separate way.

I n the twelve years during which they exhibited together, the term "Impressionism" gradually took on a precise meaning. Originally meant as ironic and even insulting, it underwent a series of changes. In 1877 it appeared in the title of the third exhibition, despite the reservations of both Renoir and Degas; to Degas especially, "Impressionism" was an empty word. Émile Zola continued to use the word "naturalism" when referring to the works of the group. By the time of the fourth exhibition, held in 1879, Degas had gained acceptance for the phrase he had been lobbying for: "Group of Independent Artists." It was used for the fourth, fifth, and sixth exhibitions. Neither the public nor the critics accepted this new name, however, and kept to the terms "Impressionism" and "Impressionists." The magazine *L'Impressioniste*, which appeared during the third exhibition, contributed to their widespread acceptance. But it was the caricatures that were published in several newspapers and incorporated into cabaret scenes and a vaudeville play that made this movement a household word in Paris.

The first four exhibitions were rejected by the critics. With the fifth exhibition, in 1881, this negative attitude evolved into a sort of condescending reserve. Impressionism had ceased to be strange and provocative, and the critics had learned to distinguish its individual forms of expression. Besides, it had influenced so-called "official" painting since 1876, when the first attempts had been made to incorporate some of its elements into academicism.

Just as the public began to take notice of Impressionism, Zola started openly opposing its adherents. In the articles he wrote about the Paris Salon in 1880, he noted that none of the Impressionists had completely and convincingly realized the new artistic concept. He saw them as merely paving the way for another new style which was still to come. In 1886, he topped this indictment of Impressionism with his novel *L'Oeuvre* (The Masterpiece), whose protagonist, Claude Lantier, was described as "a great painter who failed" and "an incomplete genius." The book was labeled a work of fiction, but almost everyone knew that Lantier was a thinly-disguised Paul Cézanne. *L'Oeuvre* led to the final break between Zola and his friends.

W hile the Impressionists' research into color and light gave modern twentieth-century painting its start, the drawings of the French Impressionists went almost unnoticed by collectors and art historians for many years. This seems understandable when we recall that the main reason the Impressionists studied light was for the oil painting. The public, however, appreciated the pastel drawings of Manet, Degas, and Renoir and the watercolors of Cézanne and Morisot as much as they did the oils; their colorfulness caught the eye. This in turn led to a more serious consideration of Impressionist drawing in general, since colorfulness is one of its characteristics.

Although the Impressionists drew with pencil, pen, and the brush, and with India ink, charcoal, and black chalk, it is important to note that they preferred colored pencils, red chalk, pastels, watercolor, and, whenever possible, gouache. These media brought their drawings closer to paintings in terms of their quality and appearance.

The Barbizon painters had opted for wash over pen-and-ink drawings and watercolors; the Impressionists favored pastels and watercolors because they seemed better suited to an art rooted in visual experiences.

From the Impressionist point of view, the point at which the form becomes blurred in the light and the atmosphere is the point at which drawing ceases to play a constructive role and colored dots become the only possible means of expression. Some of the watercolors of Pissarro, Cézanne, and Renoir clearly conformed to this theory.

The Impressionists were not interested in landscape in the sense of either realism or romanticism. They concerned themselves with the overall impression, with the emphasis on light and atmospheric conditions. Whenever possible, they painted in the open air, applying their pigments directly to the canvas without the intermediate step of drawing.

Notwithstanding this creative process, they did not totally neglect drawing. In fact, almost all known techniques can be found in the drawings they did prepare. Many made use of soft media and procedures that allowed them to easily gradate colors and dissolve outlines. Manet's ink brush and wash drawings were primarily pictorial. Renoir's works in red chalk achieved the same range of expression as Degas's pastels. And Monet gave us the consummate Impressionist drawing: an open form so bathed in sunlight that it seems to melt.

Although the Impressionist drawing most often took the form of a draft, a sketch, or a study—preparation for a painting—it eventually freed itself to become an independent artistic expression; this is most noticeable in the late works of Manet, Degas, and Renoir. Today the drawings of the Impressionists, and of Degas in particular, comprise an important part of the French tradition. When discussing the role that drawing played in Degas's work, Sir Kenneth Clark did not hesitate to call Degas the greatest graphic artist since the Italian Renaissance.

The drawings and watercolors of Auguste Rodin (1840-1917), the great sculptor and friend of Monet, are often mentioned in connection with those of the Impressionists. Although Rodin's works do not fit neatly into this category, they do possess certain features reminiscent of Impressionism. They capture the cursory and the momentary; they focus on light and illumination; they attempt to connect the plastic form with the surrounding space.

The drawings of the French Impressionists have played—and continue to play—a significant role in the world of art. Equally important, they are a virtually inexhaustible source of pleasure and of aesthetic experiences that grow richer with the passage of time. The closer we get to them, the more insight we gain into the creative genius that was their source: the genius that was shared for a brief, brilliant time by Manet and Degas, Morisot and Monet, Renoir and Sisley, Pissarro and Cézanne. Their passing impressions have become lasting treasures.

SELECTED BIBLIOGRAPHY

Introduction

Blunden, Maria and Godfrey and J.-L. Daval. *Impressionists and Impressionism*. New York: Rizzoli, 1976.

Dunlop, Ian. *The Shock of the New: Seven Historic Exhibitions of Modern Art*. New York: American Heritage Press, 1972.

The Impressionists and The Salon (1874-1886) (exhibition catalogue). Riverside: University of California, 1974.

Nochlin, Linda. *Impressionism and Post-Impressionism 1874-1904*. (From the series, Sources and Documents in The History of Art.) Englewood Cliffs, N.J.: Prentice-Hall, 1966.

Rewald, John. *The History of Impressionism*. 4th rev. ed. New York: The Museum of Modern Art, 1973.

White, Barbara Ehrlich, ed. *Impressionism in Perspective*. (From the series, Artists in Perspective.) Englewood Cliffs, N.J.: Prentice-Hall, 1978.

Essay

Ash, R. *The Impressionists and their Art*. London: 1980.

Bataille, G. *Manet*. New York: 1955.

Bell, C. *The French Impressionists*. London and New York: 1952.

Bellony-Reward, A. *The Lost World of the Impressionists*. London and Boston: 1976.

Cogniat, R. *A Dictionary of Impressionism*. London: 1973.

--------- *Monet and His World*. London and New York: 1966.

Courthion, P. *Impressionism*. New York: 1971.

--------- *Manet*. London and New York: 1963.

Denis, T. *Impressionists*. London, New York, Sydney, and Toronto: 1975.

Dunlop, I. *Degas*. London: 1979.

Fosca, F. *Renoir*. London: 1969.

Gaunt, W. *The Impressionists*. London: 1970.

--------- *Renoir*. London: 1952.

Mark, G. *Paul Cézanne*. New York: 1935.

Manson, J.B. *The Life and Work of Edgar Degas*. London: 1927.

Pach, W. *Renoir*. New York: 1950.

Pool, P. *Impressionism*. London and New York: 1967.

Rewald, J. *The History of Impressionism*. New York: 1946.

--------- *Manet: Pastels*. Oxford: 1947.

--------- *Renoir Drawings*. New York: 1948.

--------- *Pissarro*. London: 1963.

Schapiro, M. *Cézanne*. New York: 1952.

Seitz, W.C. *Monet*. London and New York: 1960.

Sérullaz, M. *Phaidon Encyclopedia of Impressionism*. Oxford and New York: 1978.

Sherman, H.L. *Cézanne and Visual Form*. Ohio: 1952.

Venturi, L. *Paul Cézanne—Water Colours*. London: 1943.

Venturi, L. *Cézanne*. London and New York: 1978.

CATALOGUE

—Cover—

Edgar Degas, DANCERS, 1899 *(see description, plate 26)*

—Frontispiece—

Claude Monet, PORTRAIT OF CAMILLE DONCIEUX, 1866-1867
(see description, plate 35)

REPRODUCTIONS IN THE TEXT

—I—

Edouard Manet, PARIS CAFÉ *(probably the Café Guerbois)*, 1869
India ink on paper, 29.5 x 39.4 cm.
Signed lower right: "Manet 1869"
Fogg Art Museum, Cambridge, Massachusetts
Bequest of Meta and Paul J. Sachs

—II—

Edouard Manet, study for BOATING
(also called BOATING AT ARGENTEUIL*), 1874*
Ink and brush on paper, 15.5 x 14 cm.
Signed lower right: "E.M."
Private collection, Paris
Study for the painting from 1874 now in the Metropolitan Museum of Art, New York.

—III—

Edouard Manet, PORTRAIT OF CLAUDE MONET, 1870s
Ink and brush on paper

—IV—

Edouard Manet, PORTRAIT OF GUSTAVE COURBET, 1878
Ink and brush on paper, 24 x 18 cm.
Signed lower left: "E.M."
Musée Courbet, Ornans
Gift of Dr. Paul Gachet

—V—

Frédéric Bazille, SELF-PORTRAIT, late 1860s
Black chalk on paper, 24.1 x 34.5 cm.
Cabinet des Dessins, The Louvre, Paris

Monet, Renoir, Sisley, and Bazille were inseparable friends; Bazille died in the Franco-Prussion War in 1871.

—VI—

Claude Monet, CARICATURE OF M. OCHARD, 1856-58
Pencil on paper, 24.1 x 34.5 cm.
The Art Institute of Chicago

As a young boy, Monet earned money drawing caricatures. Ochard was one of Monet's teachers.

—VII—

Auguste Renoir, THE JUDGMENT OF PARIS, 1908
Ocher and chalk on paper, 47.3 x 61.3 cm.
Signed lower right: "Renoir"
The Phillips Collection, Washington, D.C.

A large sketch for the painting from 1908.

—VIII—

Alfred Sisley, FARMERS AT WORK, c. 1894
Pencil and pastel on paper, 16.5 x 24.5 cm.
Signed lower right: "Sisley"
Private collection, Paris

—IX—

Alfred Sisley, THE LUMBERMILL, 1877
Pen and ink
Signed lower right: "Sisley"
Cabinet des Estampes, Bibliothéque Nationale, Paris

This drawing was published on the cover of the magazine *L'Impressioniste* on April 28, 1877.

—X—

Camille Pissarro, THE SOWER, 1860s
Pen and ink

—XI—

Camille Pissarro, HARVESTING POTATOES, 1860s
Pen and ink
Signed lower left: "C P"

—XII—

Camille Pissarro, GRAZING IN THE WOODS, 1870s
Pen and ink
Signed lower right: "C P"

—XIII—

Paul Cézanne, CAMILLE PISSARRO SEARCHING FOR A MOTIF, c. 1874
Pencil on paper, 18.5 x 11.5 cm.
Cabinet des Dessins, The Louvre, Paris
A drawing from Cézanne's sketchbook.

THE PLATES

—1—

Edouard Manet, CONCERT IN THE TUILERIES, 1860
Wash over ink on two sheets of paper glued together, 18 x 22.5 cm.
Private collection, Paris
A sketch for the painting from 1862 (London, National Gallery). The man in the white shirt
with his hand behind his back is the artist's brother Eugène; the lady sitting in front of him is
the wife of Lejosne, the commandant of the imperial guard, who introduced Manet to
Baudelaire.

—2—

Edouard Manet, SPANISH DANCERS, 1862
Pencil, watercolor, and ink with white on paper, 23.2 x 41.5 cm.
Signed lower left: "Manet"
Szépmüvészeti Muzeum, Budapest
A draft for the painting of the same name (The Phillips Collection, Washington, D.C.).
The dancers in the foreground are Lola de Valence and Camprubi.

—3—

Edouard Manet, LOLA DE VALENCE, 1861-1862
Pencil, wash over ink, and watercolor on paper, 25.3 x 17.1 cm.
Cabinet des Dessins, The Louvre, Paris

A precise and detailed sketch for the painting from 1862 (Jeu de Paume, The Louvre, Paris), it belongs to Manet's Spanish period.

—4—

Edouard Manet, FASTENING THE STOCKINGS, 1878
Pastel on canvas, 55 x 46 cm.
Museum of Ordrupgaard, Copenhagen

This work is reminiscent of Degas in both its pastel technique and its motif; the only significant difference is the artist's emphasis on brown.

—5—

Edouard Manet, study for OLYMPIA, 1863
Red chalk on paper, 24.5 x 45.7 cm.
Cabinet des Dessins, The Louvre, Paris

A composition study for the painting that created a scandal when it was exhibited in the Salon des Refusés in 1865. The final watercolor is in a private collection in London. The model was Victorine Meurent.

—6—

Edouard Manet, sketch for L'DÉJEUNER SUR L'HERBE, 1862
Pencil and watercolor on paper, 34 x 40.5 cm.
Private collection, Oxford

The definitive watercolor for the painting (Jeu de Paume, The Louvre, Paris) that created a scandal when it was shown in the Salon des Refusés in 1863.

—7—

Edouard Manet, FEMALE NUDE FROM BEHIND, 1878
Pastel on cardboard, 56 x 46 cm.
Private collection, Zürich

This distinctly pictorial drawing is also reminiscent of Degas. The long, parallel lines that define the body's form are typical of Manet.

—8, 9—

Edouard Manet, study for the etching LA TOILETTE, 1862
Black chalk on paper, 28 x 20 cm.
Courtauld Institute Galleries, London

Study for the sixth etching from a collection of eight published in 1862 by Cadart.

—10—

Edouard Manet, PORTRAIT OF BERTHE MORISOT, 1872
Pencil on paper, 17.5 x 14 cm.
Signed lower right: "E.M."
Private collection, Paris

Morisot sat for Manet between 1868 and 1872.

—11—

Edouard Manet, IRISES, 1880
Pencil and watercolor on paper, 35.5 x 24.9 cm.
Chilseldon, Wiltshire, England

Although Manet painted flowers as early as 1864, he primarily did so during the last years of his life. This watercolor was probably intended as a gift for a woman.

—12—

Edouard Manet, THE BARRICADE, 1871
Pencil and watercolor on paper, 45 x 31 cm.
Szépmüvészeti Muzeum, Budapest

A scene from the dramatic week in May of 1871 when the defenders of the Paris Commune were executed. The composition of the firing squad was taken from Manet's painting THE EXECUTION OF EMPEROR MAXIMILIAN OF MEXICO BY A FIRING SQUAD from 1867 (Kunsthalle, Mannheim).

—13—

Edouard Manet, model for BAR IN THE FOLIES-BERGÈRES, 1881
Pastel on cardboard, 54 x 34 cm.
Signed lower right: "Manet"
Musée des Beaux-Arts, Dijon

Like other pastels from Manet's late period, this is more of a painting than a drawing and gives the impression of an oil painting in its color application and hand.

55

—14—

Edouard Manet, RUE MOSNIER, PARIS, 1878
Wash over ink on paper, 28 x 43.8 cm.
Signed lower right: "E.M."
The Art Institute of Chicago

Manet loved the view from his study on the Rue Saint-Petersbourg down the Rue de Paris (today the Rue de Berne). In this picture he captured the bustling activity of the big city with its hasty passersby, coaches, and gas lights.

—15—

Edouard Manet, THE VIENNESE (PORTRAIT OF IRMA BRUNNER), 1882
Pastel on cardboard, 55.5 x 46 cm.
Signed lower left: "Manet"
Jeu de Paume, The Louvre, Paris

Confined to his bed during his last years, Manet was still able to draw with pastels until the very end.

—16—

Edgar Degas, PORTRAIT OF EDOUARD MANET, 1864-66
Pencil and wash over ink on paper, 38 x 21 cm.
Signed lower right: "Degas"
Private collection, Paris

Degas did several portraits of his friend Manet, whom he met in 1861 or 1862 in the Louvre. It is typical of Degas that he devoted most of his effort to the face, working out its expression in detail.

—17—

Edgar Degas, MANET AT THE RACES, c. 1864
Pencil on paper, 32.2 x 24.6 cm.
Signed lower left: "Degas"
Metropolitan Museum of Art, New York

Here Manet is shown as an excited spectator at the horse races in Longchamp. The elegant young lady with a lorgnette in the background frequently modeled for Degas.

—18—

Edgar Degas, AT THE MILLINER'S SHOP, 1883
Pastel on paper, 75 x 85 cm.
Signed lower right: "Degas"
Private collection

Despite Degas's attention to detail, shown by the contrasting reds and browns in the hats in the window and on the women's heads, this pastel gives more the impression of a painting than a drawing.

19

Edgar Degas, DANCER ADJUSTING HER SLIPPER, 1874
Pencil and charcoal on paper, 32.7 x 24.4 cm.
Signed lower left: "Degas"
Note, middle right: "le bras est enforce une par..."
Metropolitan Museum of Art, New York

This study emphasizes the legs and the hands while merely outlining the tutu. By striving to capture a precise movement, Degas conveys the impression of immediacy.

Edgar Degas, BEFORE THE MIRROR, 1889
Pastel on paper, 49 x 64 cm.
Signed upper right: "Degas"
Kunsthalle, Hamburg

In contrast to the drawings of Manet, the contour in Degas's pastels is nearly lost; instead, emphasis is placed on the line modeling of the volume.

Edgar Degas, WOMAN IN THE BATH, c. 1883
Charcoal and white on paper, 31 x 23 cm.
Signed lower left: "Degas"
Private collection, Paris

A drawing from the series "Suite de nuds (sic) de femmes se baignant, se lavant, se sechant, s'esseyant, se peignant ou se faisant peigner."

Edgar Degas, AFTER THE BATH, 1895-1898
Pastel on paper, 70 x 57 cm.
Signed lower left: "Degas"
Fogg Art Museum, Cambridge, Massachusetts

The pronounced hatching shows the graphic basis of the pastel; even the reflections are accentuated by white hatches. A thin brown line outlines the form of the body.

23

Edgar Degas, WOMAN BATHING, 1895-1900
Charcoal on tracing paper, 30 x 30 cm.
Signed lower left: "Degas"
Museum Boymans van Beuningen, Rotterdam

Degas often painted and drew women who were—as he put it—only occupied with their bodies. The plastic liveliness and rhythm of his nudes' full forms reveal their connections to classical art.

—24—

Edgar Degas, THREE RUSSIAN DANCERS, c. 1895
Pastel on paper, 62 x 67 cm.
Signed lower left: "Degas"
National Museum, Stockholm

When a group of Russian dancers performed in national costume at the Paris Folies-Bergère in 1895, Degas made about twenty drawings and pastels of them.

—25—

Edgar Degas, DANCER DRESSING, c. 1880
Chalk on paper, 32.5 x 24 cm.
Signed lower center: "Degas"
Notes, left center: "Soignez les bracelets; tres blanche de peau/un peu verdatre"
Szépmüvészeti Muzeum, Budapest

The detailed study of dancers' positions shows the classical methodology of Degas's creativity. Notes complete what the chalk could not capture.

—26—

Edgar Degas, DANCERS, 1899
Pastel on paper, 62 x 64 cm.
Toledo (Ohio) Museum of Art

In Degas's late pastels, contour disappears and the open form is filled with intense color. Degas was especially interested in capturing the effects of stage lighting. Both the plastic characteristics and the details are preserved. With its intense coloring and radiant shades, this pastel seems more of a painting than a drawing.

—27—

Edgar Degas, JOCKEY, 1885-1890
Chalk and pastel on paper, 32 x 24 cm.
Signed lower left: "Degas"
Private collection, Freiburg

Drawn from memory in the studio, this work was inspired by older sketches done from life. The generosity of style and a certain melancholy are characteristic of other drawings of the time, when Degas was focusing primarily on female dancers and nudes.

—28—

Berthe Morisot, WOMAN WITH CHILD ON THE BALCONY, 1872
Pencil and watercolor on paper, 19 x 15 cm.
Signed lower right: "B.M."
The Art Institute of Chicago

A pure watercolor in which the pencil drawing is lost, this preserves the charm of a color improvisation and impressive suggestion. The motif is characteristic for Morisot; this may have originally been a draft for a larger painting.

—29—

Berthe Morisot, MADAME GOBILLARD AND HER DAUGHTER PAULA, 1875
Pencil and watercolor on paper, 15 x 20 cm.
Private collection, Paris

The tea-brown and grey-green shades echoed the coloring of the Paris salons at a time when the other Impressionists' palettes were lighter and more brilliant.

—30—

Berthe Morisot, THE ARTIST'S DAUGHTER AND NIECE AT THE PIANO, 1887
Ocher and black chalk on vellum, 58.4 x 53.3 cm.
Private collection

Morisot portrayed her loved ones with natural grace and an eye toward psychological nuances. Her affection for music resulted in her organizing Sunday concerts in her Paris apartment; one of the participants was the poet Stéphane Mallarmé.

—31—

Berthe Morisot, SEATED GIRL
Pencil and watercolor

One of the artist's most common motifs is captured here as an open form that is given unity by the watercolor.

—32—

Claude Monet, BARKS ON THE SHORE, 1864
Charcoal on paper, 17 x 31 cm.
Signed lower right: "Claude Monet"
Private collection, Stamford, Connecticut

Here the exact reproduction of the form, modeled by natural light, evidences Monet's links with Realism.

—33—

Claude Monet, THE SAINT-SIMÉON FARM, before 1870
Pastel on paper, 21.5 x 30 cm.
Private collection, Giverny

This early pastel takes advantage of the dramatic contrasts between the light and the dark parts of the picture.

—34—

Claude Monet, TREE IN FRONT OF A FARM, between 1868 and 1870
Pastel on paper, 23.5 x 24 cm.
Signed lower right: "Cl. Monet"
Private collection

This pictorial early pastel partly preserves romantic elements (the dark coloring, the dramatic illumination, and the color accents) while anticipating the expressionism of Edvard Munch with its emotional mood and intensified colors.

—35—

Claude Monet, PORTRAIT OF CAMILLE DONCIEUX, 1866-1867
Red chalk on paper, 28.5 x 21.5 cm.
Signed lower left: "Claude Monet"
Private collection, New York

Doncieux, who married Monet in 1870, posed for almost all of the female figures in Monet's early compositions. This portrait study is one of the artist's most beautiful drawings.

—36—

Claude Monet, VIEW OF ROUEN, 1872
Chalk on paper, 30 x 47 cm.
Signed lower right: "Claude Monet"
Sterling and Francine Clark Art Institute, Williamstown, Massachusetts

Monet captured the town of Rouen and its cathedral's reflection in the Seine by using a gradated range of lines, thus differentiating the various areas and characterizing the rippling surface of the water and the light reflected in it.

—37—

Claude Monet, WOMAN WITH PARASOL, 1886
Chalk on paper, 53 x 41 cm.
Signed lower right: "Claude Monet"
Private collection

A draft for the painting from 1886 (The Louvre, Paris). The blowing scarf and the dress, puffed and lifted by the wind, are more impressive in the drawing than in the final oil painting.

—38—

Claude Monet, ANGLER AT THE SEINE NEAR PONTOISE, c. 1882
Chalk on cardboard, 25.5 x 34.5 cm.
Signed lower left: "Claude Monet"
Fogg Art Museum, Cambridge, Massachusetts

A study for the painting from 1882 (Museum of the Twentieth Century, Vienna). Here Monet captured the reflections of light on the rippled water in a most unique way.

—39—

Claude Monet, HAYSTACKS AT SUNSET, c. 1891
Chalk on paper, 15 x 24 cm.
Signed lower left: "Claude Monet"
Private collection

A sketch for the painting from 1891 (The Art Institute of Chicago). This belongs to a series of pictures in which Monet tried to express light and atmosphere in the shortest possible time. The mass of haystacks almost dissolves into the brilliant air.

—40—

Claude Monet, THE SEA, 1880s
Chalk on paper, 23 x 31 cm.
Signed lower right: "C.Monet"
Private collection, Bucharest

The motif from Belle-Ile-en-Mer shows Monet's dynamic hand at conveying a grand impression.

—41—

Claude Monet, BOATS ON THE THAMES, 1902
Chalk
Signed lower left: "Cl. M. 1902"
Private collection

This fragmented drawing shows one of the artist's favorite motifs and expresses the same energy found in the later London pictures.

—42—

Auguste Renoir, sketch for LISE WITH A SUNSHADE, 1867
Pen-and-ink on paper
Signed lower right: "Renoir"

Published in the book *Les Peintres Impressionistes* by Theodore Duret (Paris: 1878). The drawing and the painting were completed in the summer of 1867 in Chailly at the edge of the Fontainebleau forest. They serve as early examples of Renoir's peculiar style, newly freed from Courbet's influence. Short, parallel strokes and cross-hatches give the drawing the appearance of a painting.

—43—

Auguste Renoir, WOMEN WITH UMBRELLAS, 1879 or 1883
Pastel on paper, 63 x 48.5 cm
Narodni muzej, Belgrade

The date of origin of this drawing is not certain, but the homogeneous composition and the technique seem to indicate the later of the two proposed. The black contours of the forms, and the light coloring highlighted with pastels, preserve the freshness of the impressionism and the grace revealed in the figures, the hair, and the drawing itself.

61

Auguste Renoir, WOMAN WITH MUFF, 1884
Pen-and-ink, 45 x 29.8 cm
Signed lower right: "A Renoir"
A.S. Pushkin Museum, Moscow

Renoir made this drawing during the period when he was searching for stimulation in classicism. He depicted the young lady with inimitable ease and, with persuasive power not seen before, characterized the quality of each of the different materials.

—45—

Auguste Renoir, DANCING COUPLE, 1883
Pen-and-ink on paper, 38.6 x 18.6 cm.
Signed lower right: "Renoir"
Note under the line: "elle valsait delicamenemen abondomie entre les bras l'am
blond aux alluns de conotir"
Private collection, Philadelphia

Sketch for THE DANCE AT BOUGIVAL from 1883 (Boston Museum of Fine Arts). The models were Suzanne Valadon and Edmond Renoir, the artist's brother.

—46—

Auguste Renoir, THREE BATHERS, 1883-1885
Pencil on paper, 108 x 62 cm.
Cabinet des Dessins, The Louvre, Paris

The largest and most complete sketch for BATHERS (Museum of Art, Philadelphia), which was exhibited at the Paris Salon in 1887.

—47—

Auguste Renoir, NUDE, 1884
Pencil, red chalk, and white chalk on paper, 98.5 x 64 cm.
The Art Institute of Chicago

A study for BATHERS (Museum of Art, Philadelphia). Among the series of drawings, sketches, and studies Renoir completed in preparation for this painting, the study of the girl scooping water with her hand to splash her companions has been worked out most thoroughly. It manifests Renoir's return to classicism.

—48—

Auguste Renoir, DANCING COUPLE, 1883
Ink and brush with watercolor on paper, 47.8 x 29.7 cm.
Signed lower right: "R"
Private collection, New York

Artistically the most impressive study for the painting DANCE IN THE OPEN AIR, its models were Aline Charigot and the painter Paul Lhote.

Auguste Renoir, FEMALE NUDE SEEN FROM THE BACK, 1884
Pencil, ocher, and chalk on paper, 44.5 x 24.5 cm.
Signed lower left: "A mon ami Ch. Durand-Ruel Renoir"
Private collection, Paris

Using ocher, Renoir, the great sensualist and heir to the Mediterranean cultural tradition, rendered this perfect homage to the beauty of the female body that for him symbolized life and nature.

Auguste Renoir, WOMAN UNDRESSING, 1870s
Pen-and-ink

A typical drawing with short, parallel strokes reminiscent of Ingres, it evidences how the female nude enchanted the painter's senses.

Auguste Renoir, THE BRIDGE AT ARGENTEUIL, 1888
Watercolor on paper, 17.3 x 23 cm.
Signed lower right: "AR"
Szépmüvészeti Muzeum, Budapest

A sketch for the painting in the Mary Harriman Gallery, New York. Renoir meant this watercolor to be purely pictorial and gave effect to bright color spots, areas, and lines without using pencil outlines.

Auguste Renoir, BERTHE MORISOT WITH HER DAUGHTER, 1894
Pastel on paper, 59 x 45.5 cm.
Museé du Petit Palais, Paris

A draft for the painting of 1894 (private collection, Paris). Berthe Morisot was a close friend of Renoir. He often visited her, and occasionally he drew or painted her.

Auguste Renoir, BATHING, 1894
Pastel on paper, 55 x 46 cm.
Signed lower right: "Renoir"
Private collection, Bern

This late pastel is characteristic of Renoir at that stage of his artistic career. Using the motif of the young women in nature, he attempted to increase the intensity of the range of colors.

—54—

Auguste Renoir, DANCER, 1895
Pencil and pastel on paper, 41.5 x 30 cm.
Signed lower left: "R"
Private collection

With its sense of passionate rhythm, its glowing, soft pastel colors, and its undamped sensuality, this study stands in sharp contrast to Degas's drawings of dancers.

—55—

Auguste Renoir, PORTRAIT OF JEAN RENOIR, 1895
Pastel on paper, 53.5 x 30 cm.
Signed lower right: "Renoir"
Private collection, London

A study of Renoir's younger son, whom he often painted during his late period.

—56—

Alfred Sisley, LE CANAL DE BRISTOL, 1880s
Colored pencils on paper, 18.8 x 25.3 cm.
Note at top: "le Canal de Bristol (Effet du soir)"
Musée du Petit Palais, Paris

In this hastily outlined sketch, Sisley attempted to capture the overall impression of the evening landscape.

—57—

Alfred Sisley, GEESE
Pastel on paper, 19.8 x 30.8 cm.
Signed lower right: "Sisley"
Szépmüvészeti Muzeum, Budapest

With the typical Impressionist line, Sisley depicts nine geese in characteristic poses. The lines are broken and sensitively colored with light-reflecting violet and green.

—58—

Alfred Sisley, LE CANAL DU LOING, 1883-1885
Pencil on paper, 12 x 19 cm.
Note at top: "Canal du Loing"
The Louvre, Paris

A drawing from Sisley's sketchbook from the 1880s, in which he drew landscape motifs from around Moret and the Loing river.

Alfred Sisley, THE FERRYMAN, c. 1873
Colored chalk on paper, 29.8 x 47.3 cm.
Signed lower right: "Sisley"
Narodni galerie, Prague
The shimmering air and the reflections of the light on the water form a deep, brilliant space. The subject is reminiscent of his picture, THE SEINE AT PONT-MARLY, from 1873.

Alfred Sisley, VIEW OF MORET, c. 1895
Colored pencils on paper, 16 x 23 cm.
Signed lower left: "A.S."
Note at lower right: "Moret"
Cabinet des Dessins, The Louvre, Paris
Sisley preferred colored pencils during his late period. The village of Moret, where Sisley lived starting in 1882, was on the banks of the river Loing.

Alfred Sisley, LE CANAL DU LOING, 1880s
Black chalk on yellow paper, 18.7 x 25 cm.
Musée du Petit Palais, Paris
The fine lines of Sisley's broad hand impressively interpreted the misty early morning on the river.

Alfred Sisley, TREES ON THE SEASHORE, 1897
Colored pencils on paper, 16 x 21 cm.
Signed lower left: "Juillet 1897. A.S."
Musé du Petit Palais, Paris
In this colored sketch, completed just two years before his death, Sisley used long, loose strokes to draft the essential elements of the landscape.

Alfred Sisley, LANDSCAPE, 1880s
Colored pencils on paper, 16 x 24.5 cm.
Musé du Petit Palais, Paris
Here Sisley used thickness and sharpness of line to differentiate between the vegetation, the farm houses, and the light clouds in the sky.

—64—

Camille Pissarro, VIEW OF ROUEN, 1883
Pencil on paper, 22.5 x 29 cm.
Signed lower right: "C.P."
Note, upper right: "Vue de Rouen, iccite bon secoury 1883"
Cabinet des Dessins, The Louvre, Paris
Pissarro drew this panorama of Rouen on his first visit there in 1883.

—65—

Camille Pissarro, THE CHURCH ON WESTOW HILL, 1871
Watercolor and gouache on paper, 17 x 23 cm.
Signed lower left: "C.Pissarro"
Private collection, New York
Pissarro completed this watercolor during his stay in England, where he went in 1870 to marry Julia Vellay, the mother of his children.

—66—

Camille Pissarro, FUNERAL OF CARDINAL BONNECHOSE, 1883
Watercolor on paper, 22 x 29 cm.
Signed with pencil, lower right: "C.P."
Note with pen, lower left: "Rouen, Enterrement du cardinal Bonnechose"
Crowds of people watch a funeral procession in this pure watercolor, painted in transparent dots of color.

—67—

Camille Pissarro, SITTING PEASANT WOMAN, around 1880
Gouache on canvas, 19 x 15 cm.
Signed lower right: "C.P."
Private collection, Berlin
With its Millet-like motif and dark coloring, this gouache belongs more to Realism than to Impressionism.

—68—

Camille Pissarro, CROUCHING PEASANT WOMAN, 1878-1881
Charcoal on paper, 62 x 46.5 cm.
Signed lower right: "C.P."
Cabinet des Dessins, The Louvre, Paris
A study for the paintings from 1878 and 1881. In this drawing Pissarro attempted to differentiate the characteristics of the materials by emphasizing the constructive function of the lines.

Camille Pissarro, study for THE CAT, 1880s
Charcoal
Signed lower right: "C.P."
Cabinet des Dessins, The Louvre, Paris

These realistic studies of peasant women deal not only with their movement but also with their hairstyles and the details of their clothes.

Camille Pissarro, FRUIT MARKET IN PONTOISE, 1882
Pen-and-ink, watercolor, and gouache on paper, 31 x 24 cm.
Szépmüvészeti Muzeum, Budapest

Pissarro colored this drawing from life with broken shades that intensify its realistic character.

Camille Pissarro, PORTRAIT OF THE ARTIST'S SON RUDOLPH, c. 1885
Watercolor
Signed lower right: "C. Pissarro"
Private collection, New York

Through colored dots of watercolor applied to wet and dry areas, Pissarro captured his subject's inner self.

Camille Pissarro, study for PICKING FRUIT, 1881
Pastel on paper, 61 x 47 cm.
Signed lower right: "C.P."

A study for the painting completed during the same year (private collection, New York).

Camille Pissarro, SELF-PORTRAIT, 1888
Pen-and-ink on paper, 16.6 x 12.9 cm.
Signed lower left: "C. Pissarro 88"
New York Public Library, New York

Here Pissarro portrayed his own magnificent head and searching eyes, forever fixed on the observer.

Camille Pissarro, VILLAGER BURNING BRUSHWOOD, c. 1890
Gouache on paper, 59 x 46.5 cm.
Signed lower right: "C.P."
The Norton Simon Foundation, Los Angeles

The way in which the colors are applied—in thin, short strokes—is reminiscent of Neo-Impressionism, which Pissarro abandoned in 1888.

Camille Pissarro, VIEW OF TROYES, 1898
Watercolor
Signed lower right: "Troyes C.P."
Private collection, Paris

The pencil drawing serves as a skeleton for the colors, whose transparent shades give this scene a distinct liveliness.

Paul Cézanne, STILL LIFE WITH FRUIT, 1872-1877
Pencil and watercolor on paper, 23.8 x 31.8 cm.
Szépmüvészeti Muzeum, Budapest

This early watercolor was made as a draft for a painting.

Paul Cézanne, STILL LIFE WITH JUG, 1880s
Pencil on paper, 21 x 34.5 cm.

This incomplete study for the painting of the same name dates from the time when Cézanne first began achieving his characteristic deformation of form and composition. Parallel, broken strokes follow the form, but the jug, set at an angle, lacks contour.

Paul Cézanne, PORTRAIT OF ACHILLE EMPERAIRE, 1868
Charcoal on paper, 49 x 31 cm.
The Louvre, Paris

A study for the painting from 1869 (private collection, Paris). Emperaire was a painter in Aix-en-Provence and a friend of Cézanne.

—79—

Paul Cézanne, SELF-PORTRAIT, c. 1880
Pencil on paper, 30 x 25 cm.
Szépmüvészeti Muzeum, Budapest
This distinctly modeled head has its counterpart in another self-portrait painted around the same time (private collection, Winterthur). The drawing conveys a deeper psychological characterization than the painting, however.

—80—

Paul Cézanne, PORTRAIT OF MADAME CÉZANNE, 1883-1886
Pencil and chalk on paper, 48.7 x 32 cm.
Museum Boymans-van-Beuningen, Rotterdam
Of the many drawn and painted portraits Cézanne did of his wife, Hortense Cézanne-Piquet, this one is the most artistically impressive.

—81—

Paul Cézanne, LOVE PLAY, 1875-1876
Pencil and watercolor on paper, 22 x 15.5 cm.
Private collection, New York
A draft for the painting of the same name (private collection, New York). LOVE PLAY is from the artist's romantic period, during which he was influenced by Delacroix and Rubens.

—82—

Paul Cézanne, STUDY, c. 1882
Pencil and chalk on paper, 49.8 x 32.2 cm.
Museum Boymans-van-Beuningen, Rotterdam
A combined self-portrait, study of a sleeping boy (probably his son), and female nude after Augustin Pajou's marble statue, PSYCHE ABANDONED (The Louvre, Paris). All of these drawings are from Cézanne's mature period.

—83—

Paul Cézanne, CARD PLAYERS, 1890-1892
Pencil and watercolor on paper, 51.5 x 36.9 cm.
Rhode Island School of Design Museum of Art, Providence
A study for the painting THE CARD PLAYERS (Metropolitan Museum of Art, New York).

69

—84—

Paul Cézanne, AVENUE, c. 1888
Watercolor on paper, 48 x 32 cm.

This study probably dates from the period when Cézanne painted the avenues near Chantilly (1888) and in Jas de Bouffan (1888-1890).

—85—

Paul Cézanne, THE TREE, c. 1885-1890
Pencil on paper, 47.5 x 31.3 cm.
Narodni galerie, Prague

This study is probably related to the painting THE LARGE TREE from 1885-1887 (The Hermitage, Leningrad). Cézanne returned to this motif in a later painting from 1892-1896 (Museo de Arte, São Paulo).

—86—

Paul Cézanne, THE BLACK CASTLE AND MOUNT SAINTE-VICTOIRE,
1895-1900
Pencil and watercolor on paper, 31.5 x 48.5 cm.
The Albertina, Vienna

Mount Sainte-Victoire near Aix-en-Provence is an oft-repeated motif in Cézanne's late landscapes. The black castle was on the way to Tholonet, where the artist rented a studio between 1887-1902.

—87—

Paul Cézanne, STUDY OF PUGET'S "HERCULES," 1890-1895
Chalk on paper, 47 x 30 cm.
Private collection, London

Puget was a sculptor and friend of Cézanne; both came from Aix-en-Provence.

—88—

Paul Cézanne, STILL LIFE WITH TEA POT, c. 1900
Watercolor on paper, 47 x 62 cm.
Private collection, New York

This late watercolor, intended as a sketch for a painting, is in itself a work of art. It demonstrates Cézanne's efforts to create composition out of pure colored tones.

THE PLATES

1

3

4

13

Degas.

19

Soigner
les bracelets

très blanche de peau
un peu verdâtre

Degas

27

28

33

CL. M. 1902

elle valsait délicieusement abandonnée
entre les bras d'un blond aux allures
de cavalier.

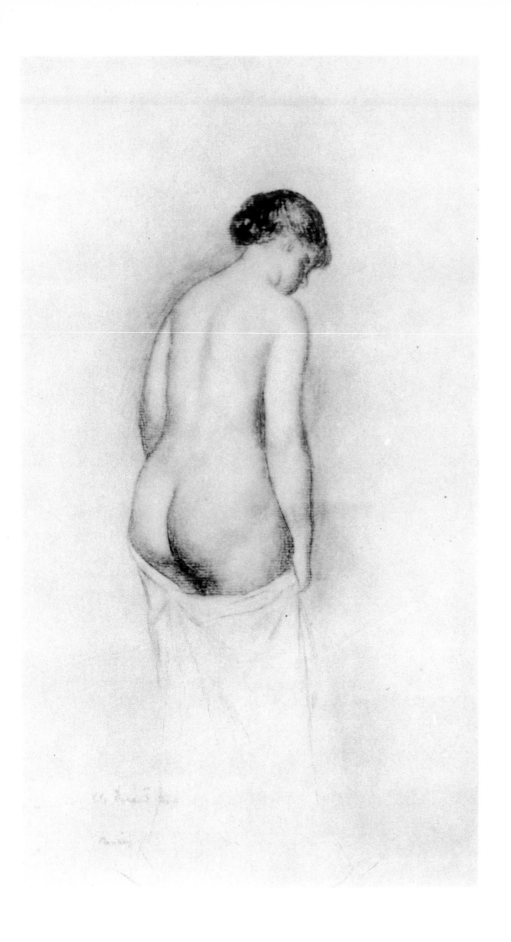
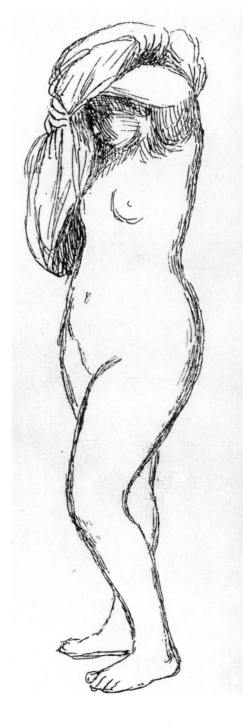

51

54

le canal de Bristol . (effet de soir)

Canal du Loing

69

C. Pissarro. 88